Vocabulary

Titles in the Resource Books for Teachers series

Beginners
Peter Grundy

Classroom Dynamics
Jill Hadfield

Conversation
Rob Nolasco and Lois Arthur

Creative Story Writing
Jane Spiro

Cultural Awareness
Barry Tomalin and Susan Stempleski

Dictionaries
Jonathan Wright

Drama
Charlyn Wessels

Exam Classes
Peter May

Film
Susan Stempleski and Barry Tomalin

Global Issues
Ricardo Sampedro and Susan Hillyard

Grammar
Scott Thornbury

Grammar Dictation
Ruth Wajnryb

Homework
Lesley Painter

The Internet
Scott Windeatt, David Hardisty, and David Eastment

Learner-based Teaching
Colin Campbell and Hanna Kryszewska

Letters
Nicky Burbidge, Peta Gray, Sheila Levy, and Mario Rinvolucri

Listening
Goodith White

Literature
Alan Duff and Alan Maley

Music and Song
Tim Murphey

Newspapers
Peter Grundy

Project Work 2nd edition
Diana L. Fried-Booth

Pronunciation
Clement Laroy

Role Play
Gillian Porter Ladousse

Vocabulary 2nd edition
John Morgan and Mario Rinvolucri

Writing 2nd edition
Tricia Hedge

Primary Resource Books

Art and Crafts with Children
Andrew Wright

Assessing Young Learners
Sophie Ioannou-Georgiou and Pavlos Pavlou

Creating Stories with Children
Andrew Wright

Drama with Children
Sarah Phillips

Games for Children
Gordon Lewis with Günther Bedson

The Internet and Young Learners
Gordon Lewis

Projects with Young Learners
Diane Phillips, Sarah Burwood, and Helen Dunford

Storytelling with Children
Andrew Wright

Very Young Learners
Vanessa Reilly and Sheila M. Ward

Writing with Children
Jackie Reilly and Vanessa Reilly

Young Learners
Sarah Phillips

Resource Books for Teachers
series editor Alan Maley

Vocabulary

Second edition

John Morgan
Mario Rinvolucri

OXFORD
UNIVERSITY PRESS

Great Clarendon Street, Oxford OX2 6DP

Oxford University Press is a department of the University of Oxford. It furthers the University's objective of excellence in research, scholarship, and education by publishing worldwide in

Oxford New York

Auckland Cape Town Dar es Salaam Hong Kong Karachi Kuala Lumpur Madrid Melbourne Mexico City Nairobi New Delhi Shanghai Taipei Toronto

With offices in

Argentina Austria Brazil Chile Czech Republic France Greece Guatemala Hungary Italy Japan Poland Portugal Singapore South Korea Switzerland Thailand Turkey Ukraine Vietnam

OXFORD and OXFORD ENGLISH are registered trade marks of Oxford University Press in the UK and in certain other countries

First published 2004
2010 2009 2008 2007 2006
10 9 8 7 6 5 4 3

ISBN-13: 978 0 19 442186 7
ISBN-10: 0 19 442186 4

Printed in China

Acknowledgements

We should like to thank the following people: students from Davies's/ Eurocentre Cambridge, the New School, Cambridge, and Pilgrims, Canterbury; the many colleagues who have supplied us with ideas, who are individually acknowledged where possible; Michael Rundell, for inspiration and practical guidance in using corpora; Catherine Robinson, who edited the first edition of the book, and Simon Murison-Bowie, who solved many of the problems thrown up by the second; our families in their participation in writing and testing.

The authors and publisher are grateful to those who have given permission to reproduce the following extracts and adaptations of copyright material:

Bereavement Publishing, Inc. (www.bereavementsources.com) for permission to reproduce the poem 'The Elephant in the room' by Terry Kettering.

Blackwell and Mott for permission to reproduce an extract from *More Grooks* by Piet Hein.

Bloomsbury Publishing, McClelland and Stewart (Canada), and Random House (Alfred Knopf) for permission to reproduce 'Fugitive pieces' by Anne Michaels.

Committee on Poverty and the Arms Trade for an extract from *Bombs for Breakfast* published by Campaign Against Arms Trade in 1978 (2nd edn.1981).

Cedric Robinson and David & Charles for an extract from *Sand Pilot of Morecambe Bay* (1980).

Daniella Cammack for an extract from an email.

David Higham Associates for permission to reproduce an extract from *The Secret Pilgrim* by John Le Carré. © 1990 David Cornwell. Published by Hodder & Stoughton, 1991.

Faber and Faber for an extract from *The Whitsun Weddings* by Philip Larkin.

Farrar, Straus and Giroux, LLC, and Faber and Faber for permission to reproduce 'Home is so Sad' from *Collected Poems* by Philip Larkin. Copyright © 1988, 1989 by the Estate of Philip Larkin.

The *Guardian* newspaper for 'Viaduct rescue' published in the *Guardian*, 23 February 1980.

Guy Browning for permission to reproduce an extract from 'You talking to me?' published in the *Guardian Weekend* section, 9 June 2001, © Guy Browning.

Hodder and Stoughton for an extract from *The Secret Pilgrim* by John Le Carré.

Julius Nyerere and Oxford University Press for an extract from *Ujamaa* (1968).

Kent Messenger Group for an extract from 'Drive-thru destroyed by inferno' from *Kent Messenger*, 15 March 2002.

Little, Brown and Co. and McIntyre Management for permission to reproduce an extract from *Gridlock* by Ben Elton.

Nicholas Brealey Publishing for permission to reproduce an extract from *Breaking through Culture Shock: What you Need to Succeed in International Business* by Elisabeth Marx. © Elisabeth Marx 1999. Published by Nicholas Brealey Publishing Limited in 1999.

Sheila Hocken and Victor Gollancz for an extract from *Emma and I* (1977).

Times Newspapers for 'Charlie Cairoli the clown dies aged 70' published in *The Times*, 18 February 1980.

Although every effort has been made to trace and contact copyright holders before publication, this has not been possible in some cases. We apologize for any apparent infringement of copyright and if notified, the publisher will be pleased to rectify any errors or omissions at the earliest opportunity.

Contents

2 Working with texts

5 Using corpora and concordances

The authors and series editor

John Morgan (1944–2004) worked in EFL from 1966 as a teacher, teacher trainer, coursebook and resource book writer, and lexicographer. He was associated with Pilgrims English Language courses from 1975. With Mario Rinvolucri he wrote *Once upon a Time* and *The Q Book*, as well as contributing to many Pilgrims publications. More recently he divided his time between teacher training and setting crosswords.

Mario Rinvolucri is founder member of the Pilgrims network and edits *Humanising Language Teaching*, http://www.hltmag.co.uk , a webzine for teachers. In addition to this title, Mario has co-authored *Letters* and *Video* in the Resource Books for Teachers series, as well as *Challenge to Think* (with Berer and Frank, OUP, 1982). A frequent contributor to *The Teacher Trainer*, http://www.tttjournal.co.uk, Mario's most recent publications are *Humanising your Coursebook* and, with Sheelagh Deller, *Using the Mother Tongue* (both with ETp-Delta, 2002).

Alan Maley worked for the British Council from 1962 to 1988, serving as English Language Officer in Yugoslavia, Ghana, Italy, France, and China, and as Regional Representative in South India (Madras). From 1988 to 1993 he was Director-General of the Bell Educational Trust, Cambridge. From 1993 to 1998 he was Senior Fellow in the Department of English Language and Literature of the National University of Singapore, and from 1999 to 2003 he was Director of the Graduate Programme at Assumption University, Bangkok. He is currently a freelance consultant. He has written *Literature*, in this series, *Beyond Words*, *Sounds Interesting*, *Sounds Intriguing*, *Words*, *Variations on a Theme*, and *Drama Techniques in Language Learning* (all with Alan Duff), *The Mind's Eye* (with Françoise Grellet and Alan Duff), *Learning to Listen* and *Poem into Poem* (with Sandra Moulding), *The Language Teacher's Voice*, and *Short and Sweet.*

Foreword

When the first edition of *Vocabulary* appeared in 1986, some of the ideas it presented seemed outlandish to many teachers. It is a measure of the success of the book that these ideas have now entered the mainstream. What was then considered 'way out' now forms part of accepted practice.

Vocabulary has played its part in the more general movement towards giving greater prominence to the teaching of vocabulary that has taken place since its initial publication.

Current thinking, based in large part on the analysis of computer corpora, has emphasized the importance of collocation, and therefore the fact that vocabulary is largely phrasal. Words hang together in typical clusters rather than exist in splendid isolation. Lexico-grammar—the zone where syntax and lexis cooperate to forge meaning—has become a key consideration in the way vocabulary is taught.

Another trend has been the revival of interest in the role of the mother tongue in the acquisition of a second language. Bilingual associations in vocabulary in particular clearly have a part to play.

Perhaps the other single most important development has been the recognition of learner differences, as evidenced through work in learning styles, multiple intelligences, and neurolinguistic programming (NLP). Learners apprehend the world differently, have different preferred modes of learning, and therefore need learning materials which take account of these differences.

Altogether we are now better placed to understand the nature and functions of vocabulary, what it means to know a word, and how best to acquire vocabulary.

This new edition builds on its former strengths by incorporating activities based on the ideas outlined above. If anything, this has tended to reinforce the beliefs of the authors that learning takes place through the personal associations formed by learners. It is 'depth of processing' that matters most. The activities included here all seek to promote the key quality of engagement. The authors have retained their freshness and originality of approach, and have again challenged teachers to renew themselves. This new edition should be at least as influential as the old one was.

Alan Maley

Introduction

Forty thousand schools, institutions, and teachers have bought the 1986 edition of this book since publication, which means that several million students will have experienced activities from its pages. Many teachers will have used it, too, and will have brought its approaches into their own teaching of vocabulary. 1986 is a long time ago, however, especially in a fast-changing field such as language teaching and learning, which is influenced increasingly by new thoughts, new practices, and new disciplines. We greatly welcomed, therefore, the invitation to revise and update this book.

But first, what was our thinking behind the first edition of *Vocabulary*? When we asked students back in the 1980s about their feelings on learning vocabulary, two-thirds of them said they were not taught enough words in class. Teachers seemed keen to teach grammar and pronunciation, but learning words—particular words that they needed in everyday life—came a very poor third. There seemed to be an assumption that it was enough for teachers to specify which words were to be learnt—the when and the how was up to the students.

Why should this be so? When we 'do' a reading passage or a listening comprehension with our students, surely we *are* teaching vocabulary? Sadly, in many classrooms this is not the case. Encountering and 'understanding' a word are seldom enough; as when we meet people, depth and interaction are necessary if the encounter is to be meaningful and memorable.

If teachers have not always recognized the need to devote time to the teaching of vocabulary, students themselves feel a very real need to devote time and effort to the process. Many students, indeed, develop their own methodologies for making words stick. Whether it is that of listening to successive news broadcasts on television or keeping words in matchboxes—examples we cited in the introduction to the first edition of this book—students intuitively bring to bear the commonsense understanding that for something to be effective it must be effective *for them*. Attention must be paid not to a generalized view of learning but to the variety of the individual process of learning. This book has grown out of our attempts to work with that process, and this second edition seeks to incorporate new understanding of the factors that influence it.

Making new

How have things changed, then, in the two decades that separate the editions of this book? We still see a need for practical activities of the kind offered here, and still hold to our view that vocabulary learning is best carried out interactively within the classroom, but we no longer feel that we are mapping uncharted waters. Many new theories and insights have emerged which have direct impact on what it is to 'know' a word. To stick with a nautical metaphor, we have in the past sailed before the wind of many new trends and ideas, and some of the new chapters in the book continue to stem from this new thinking.

One reason why some students experience language learning as a chore is because they find themselves asked to do again and again what they are already able to do with their eyes shut in their mother tongue. We strongly maintain, as we did twenty years ago, that a good second language exercise will offer the student an experience that is to some extent new, that they have never found themselves doing in their first language.

When this kind of freshness and element of surprise crops up in lesson after lesson, then the language classroom begins to be an interesting place. We also feel that a good second language activity, at least from elementary level up, is one that would also work adequately and maintain a reasonable level of interest among students if done in their mother tongue. This is why you should put this book in the hands of the teachers of the mother tongue in your staff-room.

A relationship with words

Another principle that underpins this book is the realization that *learning words is a relational process*. You could describe the process as *making friends with the words of the target language*. We do not subscribe to the view that a word is merely a 'signifier' that acts as a label for a 'signified' in the real world. It is much more than that. If a word is simply a label, why will second language learners pick up and remember one word apparently effortlessly, while another word, met at the same time and place, will be refused a place in their mind? Just as a look, a movement, a chance remark, a tone of voice, or something in the setting can influence our first impressions of a person, so our perception of a word can be affected by, for example:

— its sound
— the kinetic sensation of the lungs, throat, mouth, tongue, and nose when saying the word
— its tune
— its pitch
— its speed of enunciation
— the other word company it keeps (collocating ability and breadth)

— its spelling
— its shape on the page or screen
— conventional associations: semantic and syntactic categories to which the word appears to belong
— literary associations ('pail of water' in the context of Jack and Jill)
— the associations the word has for the individual learner
— the circumstances of meeting the word.

All these factors play a part in 'learning' a word. If you take them all into account, then meeting a word is a process of befriending, of coming to terms with a complex, self-standing reality.

We would like to round off these opening paragraphs with a paraphrase of part of Alan Maley's foreword to the 1986 edition:

The acquisition of vocabulary is:

- a branching process rather than a linear one. Words are not learnt mechanically, as little packets of meaning, but associatively;
- an intensely personal process. The associations and vibrations depend on our own past and present felt experience;
- a social process, rather than a solitary one. We expand our understanding of word meanings by interchanging and sharing them with others;
- not a purely intellectual, effortful process, but an experiential hands-on process too. An over-intellectual approach causes the language to be seen as an object, rather than to be incorporated within the subject—the learner.

New trends

In the years between the first edition of this book and today, there has been—as we have already suggested—significant work done which impacts upon the lexical component of language. This has fed into curricula and coursebooks, while mainstream teaching has been influenced by work on a host of theories: multiple intelligences, learning styles, neurolinguistic programming (NLP), and so on. It is easy, too, to forget, or not take account of, the fact that back in the 1980s computers had yet to have a major influence on our thinking. The computer explosion and the Internet have transformed the environment in which language is used and learning takes place.

These are some of the factors that have informed the updating of this book. We will conclude this introduction by summarizing under three headings how they have advanced our understanding of the teaching of words.

The relationship of the mother tongue to the foreign language

Over the past ten years the EFL community, particularly in the UK, has talked increasingly of the major importance of the mother tongue in the learning of a second language. There is a growing revolt against the belief, held by proponents of the Direct Method, that the mother tongue should be excluded from the second language classroom. In our view this revolt is common sense. In the case of adolescents and adults, the mother tongue is the launch pad for the second language. These learners naturally reference new words in second language via the mother tongue. To take an example: a 12-year-old Turk meeting the English word *house* will not go direct from his feelings about his home, from the sights and sounds of his home to *house;* he will go from the concept and feeling to the Turkish word *ev* and from there make an equivalence with *house*. This is natural, inevitable, and linguistically efficient, since *ev* is for him a brilliant, zipped-up synthesis of all his thoughts and feelings surrounding the concept of *house*.

Interestingly, the UK EFL voices who have recently advocated sensible use of the mother tongue include university academics *and* practising teachers. On the one hand you have influential writers like Professor Guy Cook from Reading University writing articles with titles like 'Is there Direct Method in our Madness?'(*EL Gazette*, Issue 239, 1999) and on the other Andrew Morris, a teacher in Bangladesh, writing what follows:

> I can't see the problem with judicious use of the students' mother tongue—especially at lower levels. ... as a learner of other languages myself I find it necessary at times to clarify a point of vocabulary or grammar in English, again especially at beginner level. It is absurd to operate all the time in a new second language, and ignore the many rich and valuable points of comparison there may be with their own.
> (ELTeCS-L Digest on the British Council website http://www.britishcouncil.org)

In Chapter 4, 'Bilingual texts and activities', we celebrate the lifting of the Direct Method ban on the mother tongue by offering you some exercises that we hope will please those of your students with strong linguistic intelligences. When we look back, we are amazed that we only included a couple of exercises in the first edition of this book which included the use of the student's mother tongue. We paid little attention to our own natural, contrastive way of learning other languages. If you find the exercises in this chapter useful and would like some more, consult the large vocabulary section in Deller and Rinvolucri 2002. (See the Annotated Bibliography at the end of this book.)

The sensory basis of both experience and vocabulary

Work with the technology offered by neurolinguistic programming has made us much more aware than we were before of the fact that it is through the five senses that we experience the external world *and* the internal world of words. Take this sentence:

The man went to the window and looked out.

Was your first 'representation' of the man, a picture, a feeling, or a sound? What sort of window was it? What sort of house? Where in the world did it happen? Did you get a feeling of the light, the weather, the temperature that day? Or was it night? Were there background noises, sounds? As he looked out, what was *out* like? Were you inside the 'space' of the scene, or did you see it as an external picture?

As we use our mother tongue we are continually making unconscious lexical choices based on sensory preferences that come from our deep programming. If you want to express the idea that you got angry you might say:

I saw red.	(visual)
I lost my rag.	(kinaesthetic)
I flew off the handle.	"
I reached screaming point.	(auditory)

All the above phrases carry the intended meaning, but they do so in sensorily very different ways. To express ourselves in language, we have no choice but to make continuous sensory choices as large areas of the language system are based on seeing, hearing, or feeling through the body. This awareness leads to a slew of emotionally apt activities in the course of which students discover a whole new area of themselves and their relationship to words. So, for example, dictate a set of words that the students have already studied and ask them to classify them into four columns:

eye	ear	bodily feeling	taste/smell

With the word *socks*, for example, in which of these columns would you get your first representation? And the word *mother*? Some people hear their mother, others know her through bodily feeling, while others get a mental picture of her. At a later stage in this exercise students compare their sensory categorization of the words dictated and the room is filled with animated, sometimes amazed voices, as they discover that their friend's sensory process is different from theirs. (Here we chose an auditory representation of the classroom process.)

There are, of course, plenty of abstract words in the language that are only etymologically sensory (*situation*, for example, from the Latin word *situs* meaning *place*) but the current meaning has come to mean something similar to *circumstance*, which in turn originally meant *what stands around*. But if you go to 6.15 you will find an activity in which the teacher dictates abstract words and the students visualize each. After the first shock of being asked to visualize a word like *integrity*, students find they can easily visualize analogues for or illustrations of abstract concepts. It is in this way that we 'domesticate' what is abstract into our own personal reality.

Neurolinguistic programming has a great deal to say about language and words that goes well beyond the sensory system but in this book we have confined ourselves to this small area of NLP's insights. To find out more, see O'Connor and Seymour 1990.

The discoveries made by corpus linguists

The growth of corpus linguistics over the past twenty-five years has led us to new ways of understanding words. We can now study them in their collocational environment, and we can do this on a massive scale and across hectares of text. We consciously realize how this colours and changes their meaning. Let us take the verb *to cause*. It turns out that this is not the neutral unbiased word you might think. According to one large corpus, ninety per cent of the things *caused* are negative:

to cause embarrassment
to cause havoc
to cause chaos
to cause distress
to cause pain to

When we first heard these facts during a presentation in 1999, given by Ron Carter, we were as surprised as he said he had been at first. He went on to add that corpus study had led him to doubt the accuracy of native-speaking introspection about words.

Another example, this time from Michael Rundell: his article 'If only they'd asked a linguist' (http://www.hltmag.co.uk, 2002) shows how wrong the UK Post Office was to re-name itself 'Consignia' some years ago. (In 2002 it decided to go back to calling itself 'The Royal Mail'.) According to the British National Corpus, the verb *consign* is massively negative through collocational association:

consign to the dustbin (6% of all occurrences, of which half were *the dustbin of history)*
consign to oblivion (5%)
consign to the scrap-heap (3%)
consign to a museum (3%)

Rundell writes, 'It is almost impossible to find a single context in which *consign* appears in a positive light'. Indeed the UK Post Office should have consulted a linguist before renaming themselves with one of the most negatively collocating words in the language!

In Chapter 5 we offer two types of exercise: one where students work with evidence from corpora, set out on the page in front of them, and the other where the students learn to use concordancing programs so they can make their own discoveries from raw data. This chapter invites you into the vast new thinking space that corpus linguists have been creating over the past twenty years.

Other changes to this edition

Readers of the first edition will notice that the book is now considerably longer, and is divided into eleven chapters instead of seven. This has enabled us to present the activities in a clearer way and we recommend a close study of the table of contents as a way of finding what you want. The inclusion of Aims for each activity should further facilitate this process. Some of the 'old favourites' have been updated with new texts and examples.

The development of the Internet has led to the inclusion of some net-related activities and to a number of variations and additions to others. Web addresses (URLS) have been provided for software sources and sites relating to dictionaries, corpora, and the like, though we cannot of course guarantee that all these URLS will remain valid. The Internet also provides us with an opportunity to establish a dialogue with you, our readers. This book is among the first to be supported by a website devoted to the Resource Books for Teachers series, to be found at http://www.oup.com/elt/teacher/rbt, and we welcome your feedback. There you will find, too, extra activities, downloadable worksheets, author articles, competitions, etc. And there is more still at the OUP Teachers' Club at http://www.oup.com/elt/global/teachersclub/.

And one other thing ...

All the materials in this book are offered as suggestions for exploration and modification by the teachers and students who might use them. We aim neither to present a method to be rigorously followed, nor to specify what to teach. We hope on the other hand to provide a rich sourcebook of ideas to be dipped into, transformed, and added to. If you would like to share your ideas and experiences, please contact us via http://www.oup.com/elt/teacher/rbt.

John Morgan
Mario Rinvolucri

1

Pre-text activities

Although vocabulary may be learnt from many sources, for the majority of students the 'reading passage' found in the coursebook or supplied by the teacher is the most usual. Such texts have the advantage that they can be specially written or adapted to suit curriculum needs, to present a steady progression of grammar and vocabulary to be learnt, to form the basis for student assessment and grading, etc. On the other hand, they cannot address the huge variety of individual student needs, even among those who are 'at the same level'. Learners differ in their experience of life, in their beliefs, in their attitude to themselves and others, in their 'learning style', in their aspirations, and in countless other ways. Many of these differences will be reflected in how, and to what extent, they will learn vocabulary from the text placed in front of them.

The activities in this chapter have two principal aims: to motivate the students to read the text, and to get them to review and organize their thoughts and language resources before reading. It should be remembered that they concentrate on vocabulary use and acquisition, not on furthering good reading habits, and that an activity that is powerful enough to enable the students to learn language from a dull text may also interfere with or swamp the reading of a rich text.

1.1 What's in the text?

Level Elementary to advanced

Time 20–30 minutes

Aims To motivate students to read a text by getting them to speculate beforehand about its content.

Materials One copy of the text for each student.

Preparation

Choose and make copies of a text and from it select five to eight items of vocabulary for presentation as a 'word rose'. (See the sample text below for the kind of text that would be appropriate at upper-intermediate level.) The vocabulary items should be neither 'context-free' (for example, structure words, neutral or very general adjectives), nor 'keywords' that would closely typify the main meaning of the text: the aim should be to allow the students a reasonable chance of coming close to the text without restricting their imagination.

Procedure

1 Put up the word rose on the blackboard.

2 Tell the students that they are going to read a text in which these words appear (not necessarily in the order presented).

3 Ask them, in groups of four, to speculate on the content of the text.

4 Give out copies of the text for comparison and discussion.

Example An example of a word rose, based on the sample text below:

signs

ignore polite

writing updated

driver carriageway

permission

Sample text **The language of road-signs**

Signs are a great way of telling people things they don't know, pretend not to know, forget or simply ignore. However, there is a problem with signs, and that is that most of them have been around for so long that we're beginning not to notice them, and for a sign that is a fate worse than death.

Signs with writing on are particularly at risk because language changes a lot faster than pictures. For example, GIVE WAY. This phrase is straight out of the era of coaches and horses with an undercurrent of gentle submission. If this sign were at a polite cocktail party it would say SWOON. These days, no one gives way unless they absolutely have to. This sign should therefore be updated to NO WAY. Or just NO.

DUAL CARRIAGEWAY is another designation straight out of the 18th century. Americans think it is as quaint as we think their turnpikes are quaint. We all know what one is, but it's very difficult to think of what else it could be called. DOUBLE LANE or BIG ROAD? The metatext of DUAL CARRIAGEWAY AHEAD is clearly CHANCE TO OVERTAKE SUNDAY DRIVER AHEAD or FAST LANE AHEAD or END OF FRUSTRATION AHEAD. Sadly, the one thing you can never, ever do with a road sign is give permission, or even imply, that you can go fast.

Even REDUCE SPEED NOW is suspect, and sounds like a driving instructor's instruction. This should be updated to SLOW DOWN NOW or, a bit oxymoronically, SLOW DOWN QUICKLY. Maybe we could have them in sequence: START BRAKING NOW. BRAKE NOW. BRAKE. FOR GOD'S SAKE, BRAKE! It's an unnecessary sign. Telling people to slow down because there's something in their way is getting perilously close to teaching them to suck eggs.

Punctuation can also drift past its sell-by date. One of the most common all-purpose signs is the exclamation mark. This is clearly the same as GOSH! It implies that something moderately interesting could happen if you're easily interested. What is needed is ****! Or something from Captain Haddock like *#@&! Because that's what we all say when we round a bend at 70 miles an hour and find a modern art installation in the middle of the road.

(Guy Browning. 'You talking to me?', *The Guardian Weekend*, 9 June 2001)

Variation

Follow 1 and 2 above, then ask the class to shout out any words suggested by the words you have written up. When you hear words that are in the text, add them to the words already on the blackboard. When you have written, say, twenty more words on the board, carry on with 3 and 4 above.

1.2 Predicting meanings

Level **Elementary to advanced**

Time **10–20 minutes**

Aims **To encourage students to work out from context the meanings of unfamiliar words.**

Materials **One copy of the text for each student.**

Preparation

Select from the text that you have chosen eight to ten words that you think will not be familiar to your students. The sample text below is an example of the kind of text you might choose.

Procedure

1 Put up the unfamiliar words on the blackboard.

2 Tell the class that you have selected the words from a text that they are about to read and give them a brief outline of its content.

3 Ask them to take a sheet of paper and rule it into two columns. They should write down each of the words on the blackboard in the left-hand column, and then in the right-hand column write three or four other words that are suggested by each left-hand word. Tell them that the words they write can be suggested by sound, spelling, possible meaning, or in any other way.

4 Ask the students, in groups of three or four, to compare what they have written.

5 Give out the text. As the students read, encourage them to work out from the context what the unfamiliar words mean, before checking with you or their dictionary.

Sample text **Magweta**

After World War II, Magweta finds itself with a small foreign exchange surplus and rudimentary armed forces and police force.

The country's economy is based on agriculture, predominantly small farms run by one family, but also including a few large estates primarily producing cash crops for export. A civilian political grouping has recently come to power with a policy of rapid industrial development, basing its appeal on nationalistic sentiment amongst the people.

To transform the country, the ruling group starts to import large quantities of machinery, including small amounts of arms, although the cost of the latter is reduced by a grant of military aid from a Western power. Many of the ruling group have been educated in the West and have acquired a Western lifestyle; they set the pace by purchasing cars, radios, and similar luxuries which others in the higher echelons then seek to acquire. The politicians make patriotic speeches which justify the expansion and re-equipping of the military.

After a few years the foreign exchange position has seriously deteriorated and a loan is obtained from the IMF. Exports are encouraged and a major effort is made to expand the production of cash crops through the use of improved agricultural techniques. Selective restrictions are placed on imports in order to stimulate local production but arms imports continue to increase.

Although there is a short-term improvement helped by some direct foreign investment, a steady decline in the price of cash crop exports, relative to manufactured imports, results in a second application for a loan. This is granted on condition that the currency is devalued and import restrictions removed. This the government reluctantly accedes to.

The result of this policy is the destruction of embryonic local industry as large foreign concerns, relying heavily on advertising and the lure of Western image, flood the market. Several large tracts of land, some of which were previously farmed under the traditional system, are bought up by a few individuals and firms and converted to produce more crops for export. Employment in traditional agriculture stagnates, and the most vigorous young people leave the land to move into the urban areas where most of the wealth is concentrated. Rural society declines and shanty towns grow in the shadow of the westernised cities.

(*Bombs for Breakfast*, Campaign Against the Arms Trade, 1981)

1.3 Predicting words

Level Intermediate to advanced

Time 20–25 minutes

Aims To review areas of vocabulary with which the students already have some familiarity, so that new items in these areas can more easily be 'slotted in' and remembered; to stimulate interest in a dull text.

Materials One copy of the text for each student.

Preparation

Choose a text with a fairly narrow and predictable set of vocabulary, by virtue of its content and/or style. Examples of suitable texts might be:

- advertisements
- passages from coursebooks
- news items with a well-known theme (arms talks, earthquakes, sports reports)
- fairy stories and folk tales known to the students (for example, Cinderella, Washington and the cherry tree, Nasreddin stories)
- instructions, recipes, product descriptions
- popular songs

The sample texts below provide examples.

Procedure

1 Tell the students that later in the lesson they will be reading a text/listening to a tape/hearing a story. Give them a very rough idea of what the piece will be about: for example, in the samples below, tell them they are going to read a short article about the stresses of working for an international company/hear an American cowboy song about whisky.

2 Ask the students, in pairs, to predict some of the vocabulary they might encounter in the text. Tell them to produce a list of eight to ten items. Allow dictionaries and give assistance when asked.

3 Ask the students to form larger groups (eight to twelve) and explain their lists to one another.

4 Give out the texts/play the recording/tell the story.

Sample texts

The international commuter

An interview with a 'Euro flyer' who commutes between the UK and the continent every week shows the special challenges. This manager gave the following account:

'I feel I can cope with the demands of being in different places all the time. I have always been able to work strange hours and to juggle a lot of balls in the air, but I can also see that my family needs more reassurance. They find it probably more difficult to cope with my frantic life. In terms of the company, I would have expected more support. They do not realize the effect of short-term international travel, despite being an international company. Ideally, I would expect from my company more flexibility but also more trust. I would expect the company to treat me as a mature individual.

'What helped me personally to adapt to short-term international work are the following personality characteristics: independence, self-discipline, cultural sensitivity, being open and light-hearted, being positive, being assertive, and not being arrogant but humble.

'My career expectations have completely changed as I now think much more globally. I think nothing of picking up the phone and arranging a meeting in another country or on another continent, whereas before this it would never have occurred to me. The only negative effect of my frantic lifestyle is that I have become much more aggressive and less patient and people have in fact commented on this. I do believe I have become less tolerant of people who want to waste time and in such situations my temper has become shorter. On the other hand, I believe I have developed a deeper and better understanding of people.

'Another area that I need to guard for my own development is the private life/professional life distinction. Because I have a highly stressful international job, I find it difficult to switch off and therefore my lifestyle has become extremely pacey and adrenalin-driven. I now find it quite hard to slow down in my personal life and I want to pack in all the social activities in a very short space of time. There is definitely not enough balance in terms of relaxation in my life. This is obviously a risk in terms of long-term stress but it also puts a certain pressure on my personal relationships.'

(Elisabeth Marx. *Breaking through Culture Shock*. London: Nicholas Brealey Publishing, 1999)

Rye whiskey

I'll eat when I'm hungry,
I'll drink when I'm dry;
If the hard times don't kill me,
I'll lay down and die.

Beefsteak when I'm hungry,
Red liquor when I'm dry,
Greenbacks when I'm hard up,
And religion when I die.

They say I drink whiskey,
My money's my own;
All them that don't like me
Can leave me alone.

Sometimes I drink whiskey,
Sometimes I drink rum;
Sometimes I drink brandy,
At other times none.

Jack o' diamonds, Jack o' diamonds,
I know you of old.
You've robbed my poor pockets
Of silver and gold.

Oh, whiskey, you villain
You've been my downfall.
You've kicked me, you've hurt me—
But I love you for all.

Rye whiskey, rye whiskey,
Rye whiskey, I cry.
If you don't give me rye whiskey,
I surely will die.

(Traditional US cowboy song)

Variation

A Polish colleague, Malgorzata Szwaj, suggests putting up the first part of the title of the piece, and then asking the class to suggest ways of completing it, and what their suggested titles might refer to.

1.4 Criminal records

Level **Elementary to advanced**

Time **30–40 minutes**

Aims **To focus the students' attention on the ways they associate words by meaning or context, and especially on the positive and negative connotations words have for them.**

Materials **One copy of the text for each student.**

Preparation

Choose the key words from a text.

Procedure

1 Write up on the blackboard a skeleton 'criminal record card' of the type shown below (column 1 only).

2 Fill in an example 'criminal record' as in column 2.

3 Point out that words could also be said to have criminal records, and give a fairly concrete example in column 3:

1	2	3
Name	John Smith	*fat*
Place of residence	3 Packer Street, West Croydon	*body*
Known associates	Peter Jackson, Arthur Baines	*carbohydrates, cholesterol*
Criminal record	robbery, terrorism, kidnapping	*heart disease ugliness*

4 Write up on the blackboard the list of words from the text you have chosen. For the intermediate text overleaf this could be:

land value
belong rent
market commodity

5 Ask the students to make out 'criminal record cards' for each of the words you have written up.

6 Ask the students to form small groups (three to five) and tell each other what they have written and why.

7 Ask the class to read the text.

8 As a follow-up, they might like to consider whether they have changed their minds about any of the words after reading them in context.

Examples In one group, students produced the following three examples:

Name	value	commodity	rent
Place of residence	jewellery, safe	shop	Cambridge
Known associates	money, investment	sell, buy	landlady
Criminal record	stealing, cheating	greed	dirty room, bad food

Sample text **Land**

To us in Africa land was always recognized as belonging to the community. Each individual within our society had a right to the use of the land, because otherwise he could not earn his living and one cannot have the right to life without also having the right to some means of sustaining life. But the African's right to land was simply the right to use it; he had no other right to it, nor did it occur to him to try and claim one. The foreigner introduced a completely different concept—the concept of land as a marketable commodity. According to this system, a person could claim a piece of land as his own private property whether he intended to use it or not. I could take a few square miles of land, call them 'mine', and then go off to the moon. All I had to do to gain a living from 'my' land was to charge a rent to the people who wanted to use it. If this piece of land was in an urban area I had no need to develop it at all; I could leave it to the fools who were prepared to develop all the other pieces of land surrounding 'my' piece, and in doing so automatically to raise the market value of mine. Then I could come down from the moon and demand that these fools pay me through their noses for the high value of 'my' land—a value which they themselves had created for me while I was enjoying myself on the moon! Such a system is not only foreign to us, it is completely wrong.

(Julius K. Nyerere. *Ujamaa.* Oxford University Press, 1968)

1.5 Ungrammatical gender

Level **Intermediate to advanced**

Time **30–40 minutes**

Aims **To encourage students to explore their preconceptions about particular words before meeting them in a context, so that their reading becomes more directed and critical.**

Materials **One copy of the text for each student**

Preparation

Choose a text and list 10–12 words and phrases in it that the class are likely to find hard. In the following example text these could be, for intermediate learners:

rush-hour	crowded	car chases	traffic lanes	pavement	alleyways
performing	sit up and beg	display	ploughing	equation	jam

Procedure

1 Put up your list on the blackboard and ask the students to check (with dictionaries, from each other, or by asking you) that they understand all the words.

2 Ask the students, working individually, to divide the words into male and female. Tell them that this has nothing to do with ideas of grammatical gender or 'dictionary meaning' but should express their own *feelings* about the words.

3 Invite the students to discuss in pairs why they sexed the words as they did.

4 Give out the text for the class to read.

5 Ask them to discuss in pairs if the context has led them to change their minds about any of the words and phrases.

Example Here is what one student produced:

Male	**Female**
rush-hour	pavement
car chases	traffic lanes
sit up and beg	crowded
equation	alleyways
performing	jam
display	
ploughing	

Sample text **Movie chase**

All week people sit in traffic jams. Sometimes, on a Friday night, they go to the movies. On the way they sit in more traffic jams, they miss the first part of the movie because they can't find a parking place. Then they sit in a dark cinema and watch a man drive a car through rush-hour traffic, clear across a city at eighty miles an hour. If the man had turned into a six-foot banana we would say it was a stupid movie, but a man driving a car through a crowded city at eighty miles an hour we not only accept but remark to each other how brilliantly done the car chases were.

Nothing can stop the hero in his car. If he meets another car, he drives round it, or maybe over it, or just possibly through it. He goes on the pavement, he crosses into opposing traffic lanes, he hurtles down empty alleyways. His car can jump, his car can roll over, it is more like a performing dog than a ton and a half of lifeless metal. If you offered it a biscuit it would probably sit up and beg.

The fact that this display … was shot at 5.30 a.m. on four successive Sunday mornings, means nothing. The fact that if you actually tried any of that stuff for real you would not get twenty yards before ploughing into a bus queue and killing thirty innocent pedestrians, is not part of the equation. The fact that Moses may have been able to part the Red Sea but could not do more than ten miles an hour in London, doesn't matter. Movie car chases remind us of how much we love cars.

When the movie is over, everybody goes and sits in a jam again.

(Ben Elton. *Gridlock*. Macdonald, 1991)

Comments

Many teachers might be horrified at the idea of encouraging students to associate English words with gender—it's hard enough to stop Gaston saying 'When I picked up the cup, she broke.' But quite apart from the grammar, many words are, for some of us at least, gender-loaded.

1.6 Look, remember, and complete the set

Level Elementary to advanced

Time 30–40 minutes

Aims To focus the students' attention on how they try to remember words, and on how context might influence their memory.

Materials One copy of the text, and one copy of the 'word jumble' for each student.

Preparation

From a narrative or descriptive text which you wish the class to read, select 25–30 of those vocabulary items which for you best reflect the mood and action of the passage. Set out the words you have chosen as a word jumble like the one below, which is taken from the sample text, and prepare sufficient copies for each person in the group.

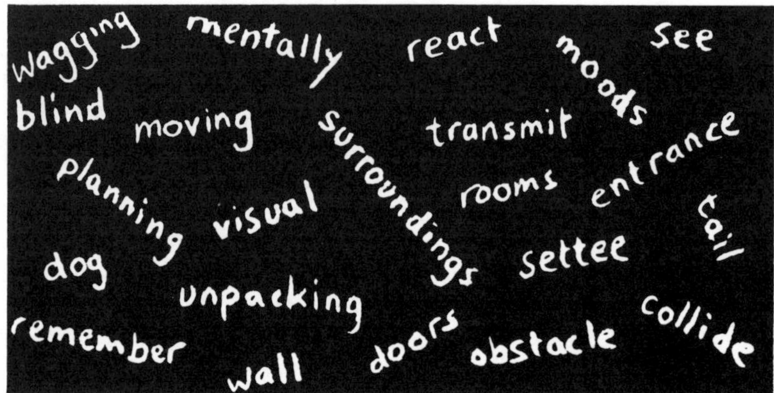

Procedure

1 Give out the word jumbles face down to each member of the group.

2 Tell the class that they will have 15 seconds (or more if you have chosen a long list) to look at the jumbles, then tell them to turn over their sheets and read.

3 When the time limit is up, tell the class to turn the jumbles face down again. Then ask them, working individually, to write out all the words they can remember.

4 Then ask them to write down any more words they think might fit the scene or action suggested by the words they have remembered. They could use a different coloured pen for this.

5 Ask the students to discuss in pairs the words they have written down, and the text they imagine contains them.

6 Give out copies of the text.

7 When the students have finished reading the text, ask them to discuss in groups of three to five a) which words they found hard to remember in step 3, and b) which words they think they will now remember, and why.

Sample text **Moving house**

It took the upheaval of moving house to bring home to me again that I could not see. This may sound odd. But having Emma I could see: not in a visual sense, obviously, but I knew what was going around me as she reacted to her surroundings. All her feelings and moods transmitted themselves through the harness. I could always tell if there was an obstacle ahead because of the way she slowed up and hesitated ever so slightly. I knew when we were passing another dog, because I could feel her looking, and her tail wagging.

But around the house it was different. Moving in a room, or from one room to another, a blind person is always mentally planning. And moving to a new house, you have to start all over again. Don helped me move in, and we had a hectic time: he put up curtain rails and changed electric plugs, while I carried on the endless business of unpacking. Emma and I collapsed into bed at about two in the morning. In next to no time, it seemed, I heard someone knocking outside (it was, in fact, Don) and I quickly got out of bed. Then I realized I could not remember exactly where the door was. I felt I was in a fitted wardrobe. After trying another wall, and coming back again to the fitted wardrobe, I finally found the right door. Pausing only to collide with the settee that I had forgotten had been put in the middle of the living room, I got to the front door. There was no one there. Then I remembered there was a back door as well, where Don was patiently waiting. It took me a long time to become accustomed to all the different doors, after being used to my flat with its one entrance and fewer rooms.

(Sheila Hocken. *Emma and I*. Gollancz, 1977)

Acknowledgements

This idea was suggested by a picture recall exercise presented by Alan Maley at the IATEFL Conference in December 1979.

1.7 Words on a map

Level **Intermediate to advanced**

Time **20–30 minutes**

Aims **To motivate and focus the students' reading of a text by first exploring the personal connections of some of the words and phrases used.**

Materials **One copy of the text, and one copy of a map or drawing, for each student.**

Preparation

Choose a passage and pick out 10–12 words and phrases from it to focus on. For the passage given below, we suggest these:

variations	to run into
component	mobility
to generate	daring to change
experiment	justifications
in one's own voice	standard rules

Choose an image (a map of a well-known country, picture of a well-known person, a symbol) and be ready to show it to the students, for example:

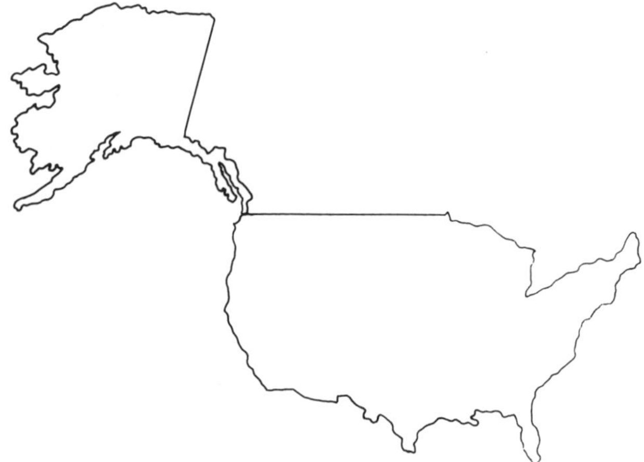

Procedure

1 Show the class the image and give them the list of words. Ask them to decide individually which words apply in some way to the image. Alternatively, give out copies of the image and ask them to write the words on it in appropriate positions.

2 Ask them to compare notes with their neighbours.

3 Give out copies of the text.

Sample text **Children at play**

Watching children play, I decided that if one presents young children with the components of games, they will generate games themselves. Children experiment with different ways of doing things, whereas adults get accustomed to believing there is one right and one wrong way to do things. Creating a game is much like discovering how to write in one's own voice. Making games, writing, building are all ways young people can discover that they can put things into the world, that they can have some control over life.

The other day I ran into some children who were playing their own version of chess. The knights jumped two squares at a time, since they galloped like horses. The queen, rooks, pawns and bishops moved in their regular ways, though the king was given the mobility of a queen. When I came upon the game a young student was telling the kids how wrong they were in daring to change the rules of the game, that they would never be 'real' chess players if they didn't play the rules. One of the kids said she didn't want to be a real chess player but was curious about what happened when you changed the rules. The new game was interesting but the student teacher insisted it wasn't a game and forced the kids to play by the standard rules. When I mentioned to him that there were dozens of variations of chess played throughout the world, he claimed that the only justification for letting children play games in school was to accustom them to learning to play by the rules. I disagree.

(H.R.Kohl. *Writing, Maths and Games.* Methuen, 1977)

1.8 Cards on the table

Level **Intermediate to advanced**

Time **20–30 minutes**

Aims **To get the students to clarify their ideas about a topic or attitude before reading a text, especially one that will be used as the basis for discussion or essay-writing.**

Materials **One copy of the text for each student; one set of 24 word cards for each group of six to eight students.**

Preparation

1 For the first class: prepare a set of 24 cards, each bearing a different word. Choose the words from a fairly well-defined area of human concern, for example:

Things and ideas close to the individual

man	animal	enemy	boy	mind	father	child	pet
son	soul	family	baby	friend	heart	daughter	mother
god	stomach	group	head	woman	girl	adult	blood

Social concerns and ideas

home	school	neighbourhood	nest	friends	garden	house	language
nation	estate	conversation	property	land	flat	society	country
speech	hospital	institution	belongings	family	wife	cottage	locality

2 For later classes: choose a passage, preferably one expressing a strong theme or point of view, and pick out 24 words and/or phrases from it which typify its content. Prepare a set of 24 cards, each bearing a different word or phrase, for every six to eight students in the class. From the text below, we have selected these:

1.8

threat	school	psychiatrist	police	nursed	neighbour
home	perpetrated	suicide	ill	teenager	mother
statistics	social services	hospital	mentally	shop	theft
refuge	magistrate	community	accused	vandalism	anorexia

Alternatively, you could dictate the list to your students and get them to prepare their own cards.

Procedure

Lesson 1

1 Arrange the classroom so that the group(s) of students can stand round a table or tables.

2 Lay out a set of cards face up in random order on the table(s).

3 Ask the group(s) to arrange the cards in groups of three (or four, or six) according to meaning. Stress that a) the group must agree unanimously and b) all the cards must be used.

4 Invite the group(s) to justify their card arrangement. If there is more than one group, get them to circulate and see what other groups have done.

Lesson 2

Follow the same procedure as above, but use cards bearing words derived from a text. The students may read the text before working on the cards, afterwards, or both. The exercise can thus be used as a lead-in to a text and/or as a way of passing comment on it and stimulating criticism and discussion.

Sample text **My mother**

About five years before her death my mother ceased her threats of suicide and embarked on a life of persistent theft. It must have been a sweet moment when a shop assistant I had once fined in the magistrate's court for shoplifting asked: 'What are you going to do about your mother's shoplifting?'

The local shops frisked my mother's pockets and shopping bag, but never bargained for the capacity of directoire knickers with strong elastics. So she still got away with a great deal, although once she shed onions and carrots as she walked.

'You mustn't do that sort of thing,' said the psychiatrist, now being chased up by the police and the social services. She was now in deep depression at being accused of stealing, and he took her into hospital for a course of electro-convulsive therapy. It lifted the depression and she was quite a happy shoplifter, and the only place she was safe in was the bank.

Next came illegal entry. She would go into houses and take anything portable. During the hours of darkness my mother, then 83, fell over a wall between two houses, suffered appalling lacerations, and left a trail of blood back to her home.

'Now they will be obliged to take her in!' said the GP. With a suitcase in the boot I drove her to the clinic.

'You have made a mess of yourself,' said the psychiatrist. I drove her home—my home—and nursed her for six weeks.

With great resilience she became as active as ever, and the community was beset by teenage vandalism. The police visited schools, and my mother's neighbour, after several bouts of damage, bought a huge Alsatian, which, he assured me, would tear to pieces anyone who touched the car.

Watchers, some time after that, witnessed the car vandalism. My mother selected the car, went into the house for an instrument, and perpetrated the damage. A frustrated policeman told me: 'And to cap it all, the ruddy dog was helping her!'

'This time she will be taken in,' said both GP and social workers, but she was not. Her last refuge was anorexia nervosa.

'It is time you had some relief,' the psychiatrist told me. He proposed taking her into the psycho-geriatric ward for three weeks.

Before that time came she had another fall. Lacerated and shocked, she was taken into the local general hospital. The following morning I was told by the ward sister that she was much improved, and eating her breakfast as if she had not seen food for a month. A few minutes later she rang back. My mother had choked to death. She had joined the statistics of those mentally ill who are successfully maintained within the community.

(Clarice Maizel. 'A little old thief', *The Guardian*, 19 December 1983)

Comments

The activity can also be used after reading a text, as a way of expressing the reader's understanding or reaction.

2
Working with texts

As in the previous chapter, we are concerned here with the use of texts as a source of vocabulary and as an aid to learning vocabulary: we are not offering strategies for efficient reading. For that reason, we concentrate on shorter texts, which can be worked through during a single class session, and have also included activities that can be used with oral texts (for example, 2.3, 'Correct the teacher', and 2.13, 'Be someone else'). The emphasis throughout is on getting the students to connect the words and phrases they meet in the text with what they already know, and with their own experience of life and language (for example, 2.9, 'The words in your past').

The context in which one meets a word or phrase is important in establishing its exact meaning and connotation, and due attention is paid to this throughout, but it is also important in terms of memorability—an item met in one context may be remembered, in another forgotten. This applies also to the 'context of situation'—the setting (place, people, mood and so on) in which the text is read/heard and discussed. To this end, we have tried to make activities that are both interactive and memorable in themselves.

Many of the activities in this chapter include 'sample texts'. These are intended purely as examples, to make the instructions more concrete and to give the teacher and students a ready-made package with which to try out the core ideas. Choosing your own texts, or getting the students to choose them, will almost always be preferable. For this reason, we have avoided designing activities round specific texts, and in those few cases where instructions relate to specific features of a sample text (for example, 2.14, 'Email language': '4 Ask them to make a list of all the two- and three-part verbs.'), it should be a simple matter to substitute a task based on the actual text you are using.

2.1 Customizing a text

Level Intermediate to advanced

Time 20–30 minutes

Aims 1 To focus the students' attention by giving them a specific task, rather than simply telling them to read the text.

2 To encourage them to look closely at words and phrases in context.

Materials **One copy of the text, and one copy of the 'Alternative words' sheet, for each student.**

Preparation

From the next reading passage you propose to use with your class, select 10–15 words and phrases to focus on. Write these down. Then prepare a sheet of 25–40 different words and phrases (not only synonyms) from which alternatives to those in the text can be chosen. (See the example below, at intermediate level.)

Procedure

1 Give the students the reading passage to look through.
2 Slowly say the words and phrases you have chosen while the students underline them in the passage.
3 Give out the sheet of alternative words and phrases.
4 Ask the students to select substitutes from the sheet for the words underlined.
5 In pairs the students look at and discuss each other's choices.

Sample text **Separation**

I was about to start my second year of university and was determined to be on my own, a fact my mother had refused to accept all summer. One sun-worn August morning I carried my boxes of books down to the damp coolness of the cement parking garage and loaded up the car. My mother retreated behind the closed door of her bedroom. Only when I'd carried out the last box and was really leaving did she emerge. Grimly she prepared a parcel of food, and something was lost between us, irrevocably, the moment that plastic bag passed from her hand to mine. Over the years, the absurd package—enough for a single meal, to stop hunger for a second—was handed to me at the threshold at the end of each visit. Until it hurt less and less and the bag was simply like the roll of candy my mother passed to me from the front seat on our Sunday drives.

The first night in my own apartment, I lay in bed only a few miles across town and let my mother's phone calls ring into the dark. I didn't call for a week, then weeks at a time, though I knew it made them ill with worry. When I finally did visit, I saw that, though my parents continued in their separate silences, my defection had given them a new intimacy, a new scar. My mother still bent towards me with confidences, but only in order to withdraw them. At first I thought she was punishing me for her need of me. But my mother wasn't angry. My efforts to free myself had created a deeper harm. She was afraid. I believe that for moments my mother actually distrusted me. She would begin a story and then fall silent. 'It's nothing that would interest you.' When I protested, she suggested I go into the living room and join my father.

(Anne Michaels. *Fugitive Pieces*. Bloomsbury Publishing, 1997)

Words and phrases for dictation (in the order they appear in the text):

was determined
on my own
retreated
emerge
irrevocably
absurd
worry
intimacy
free myself
created a deeper harm
protested

Alternative words sheet

Alternative words and phrases (in random order):

without changing rejection had made up my mind hurt her more alone come out caused more serious damage useless break away show herself familiarity for ever attachment ridiculous hid refused develop withdrew had decided escape permanently independent anxiety closeness objected fear understanding

Variation

In step 4 above you can, of course, allow the students to substitute items not on the sheet. This gives them more freedom, but may also restrict their choice to what they already 'know they know', instead of leading them to explore other possibilities.

Acknowledgements

This derives from an idea proposed by Gail Moraro, an Adult Migrant Education teacher in Melbourne, in *ESL Teachers' Exchange*, December 1983.

2.2 Favourite phrases

Level **Beginner to advanced**

Time **15–30 minutes**

Aims **To give students a chance to share their feelings about vocabulary and, perhaps, overcome personal dislikes.**

Materials **Coursebook.**

Procedure

1 Deal with the coursebook unit text in your normal ways, and then ask the students to work on their own and underline three or four phrases or words in the text that they specially like.

2 Ask students to read out a phrase they like and then explain their reasons (in a beginners' class this will happen in the mother tongue). Ask if anybody else underlined the same phrase. Ask them for *their* reasons: it is the students' own preferences, not yours, that determine how deeply they can extract meaning from a text.

3 Repeat the process with 10–15 students.

Variation

Ask half the class to underline phrases and words they do *not* like, while the others underline ones they do like.

Acknowledgements

We learnt this simplest of techniques from Lonny Gold, and have used it with grumpy teenagers, with illiterate adult immigrants, with English for teachers courses. We haven't had it fail yet! Thank you, Lonny.

2.3 Correct the teacher

Level Elementary to advanced

Time 25–35 minutes in the first lesson and 45–60 minutes in the second.

Aims
1. To give a task-based focus to listening.
2. To encourage students to build up a wider set of vocabulary choices.

Materials One copy of the text and one word card for each student.

Preparation

Write out an anecdote in short sentences. Pick 10–15 words from it that you want the students to focus on and write paraphrases of them. Substitute your paraphrases for the words in the text, then write out the original words on cards to be given out to the class. You will need one card for each student, so if you have picked out ten words and your class is thirty strong, put each word on three cards.

The Sample text provides an example anecdote incorporating paraphrases.

Procedure

Lesson 1

1. Read the story once through so the students get the outline of it.
2. Give out the cards to the students. Give them a chance to check that they know the meaning of the words on them.
3. Tell the class that you are going to read the story again, but that this time they should stop you as soon as they hear a paraphrase of a word they have on their cards. After stopping you they are to repeat your sentence, substituting the word on their card for yours.
4. Read through the story again.

Lesson 2

Once your students have done two or three exercises like the one above, ask them to produce anecdotes of their own:

1. Put the students in groups of three and ask each group to write an anecdote of their own.

2 Ask the groups to prepare 6–12 paraphrases of interesting words in their texts and to put these on cards or slips of paper.

3 Ask each group of three to join with another group.

4 Within each pair of groups, ask one member of group A to read her/his group anecdote slowly to the members of group B. The cards should then be given out to the members of B and the activity proceeds as in the first class (above).

5 Repeat the activity, using group B's anecdote.

Sample text He was a hefty man in his mid-fifties. He had a large *stomach* which looked just right behind the wheel of his 30-ton *lorry*.

One day, driving along a *bendy* country road, he saw a bridge over the road ahead of him. 'Maximum height: 14ft' he read on the *notice*.

He *stopped* and *got out*. He looked from his lorry to the bridge, scratching his head *thoughtfully*.

'My lorry's 14 feet 1 inch,' he thought to himself, 'never get through there.'

Just at that moment a motor-bike *policeman* roared up and asked what the *problem* was.

'Can't get through,' the trucker told him.

'Easy,' said the other. 'Just let your tyres down an inch or two and have them *re-inflated* on the other side.'

The driver thought about this *attentively* for several minutes. 'No use,' he said *weightily*, 'it's at the top it won't get through, not at the bottom.'

The original words are put on cards for the students:

Paraphrases in text	Original words on cards
stomach	paunch
lorry	truck
bendy	twisting
notice	sign
stopped	pulled up
got out	climbed down
thoughtfully	pensively
policeman	cop
problem	trouble
re-inflated	pumped up again
attentively	carefully
weightily	ponderously

Variation

With beginners and very elementary students, give out copies of the text, then simply dictate some words extracted from it: they should underline the words they hear. In a later class, mix in a few paraphrases of words or phrases in the passage.

Acknowledgements

We owe this activity to Lou Spaventa.

2.4 Deleting Words

Level Post-beginner to advanced

Time 15–20 minutes

Aims To focus on whether a word is necessary or not as a way of exploring its meaning in context.

Materials Coursebook.

Procedure

1 Ask the students to re-read a passage from the coursebook two or three units back.

2 Tell them that texts are often improved and given more impact by cutting words out. Ask them to underline 10–12 words in the passage that they feel can usefully go, noting any grammatical changes that might also be necessary. The students work on this task in pairs.

3 Group the students in sixes to read their reduced version of the passage.

4 Share with the class the words you think are best left out and briefly explain why. Give them an opportunity to (dis)agree with you.

Variation

Working individually, students write a short composition. They then pair off and swap compositions. Student A deletes all the unnecessary words in B's work and vice versa. They come back together to discuss the deletions.

2.5 Marginalia

Level Intermediate to advanced

Time 20–45 minutes, depending on the texts chosen.

Aims To get students to look closely at vocabulary in context, and to express their own understandings of specific meanings and connotations.

Materials A different text for each group of students: five copies of each text.

Preparation

1 Choose a number of short but complete texts: poems are ideal. You will need a different text for each group of students.

2 Make copies of each text: one for each member of the group plus one additional copy.

Procedure

1 Ask the students to form groups of four members. Make sure each group has access to at least one dictionary.

2 Give one copy of the first text to group A, one copy of the second text to group B, and so on.

3 Tell the students to read and discuss their text within the group. Say you are available to answer simple questions about language, but you would prefer them to find out from each other or from the dictionary.

4 After ten minutes, ask each group to divide up their text so that each member chooses a different word or phrase from it. Not every word or phrase in the text need be chosen.

5 Give out the remaining copies of the texts, so that each student has his/her own copy.

6 Ask the students to underline, on their own copies, the word or phrase they have chosen, and then, in the margin, to make a comment on it. Explain that this can take any form they like: a paraphrase, an example sentence to show how it can be used, a response or criticism, a better alternative, even a picture.

7 Tell the students to circulate their texts around the group and to read each other's 'marginalia'.

Variation

The same activity works well with texts generated by the students themselves.

Follow-up

'Publication' is an excellent way to encourage students to respect and enjoy both their own work and that of others:

1 Put all the marginalia for each text on a sheet of paper together with the original text and make enough copies for the whole class to read.

2 If you and your students are familiar with, and have access to, computers and browser software, make a simple website for each text: the original text should be on one page (or as the main frame of a page) with each selected word or phrase made into a link and the comments to it placed in a separate page (or frame) to be displayed when the link is clicked.

2.6 Hunt the misfits

Level **Intermediate to advanced**

Time **20–35 minutes**

Aims **To develop students' critical awareness of meanings in context in a light-hearted way.**

Materials **One copy of the original text and one copy of the doctored text for each student.**

Preparation

Choose a short passage you think will be easy for your students. Change some of the words in it so that it no longer makes proper sense.

In class you will need copies of both the original passage and the doctored one. (See the Sample texts overleaf. For the second, you will need to make your own doctored version.)

Procedure

1 Give the students a copy each of the doctored text and ask them to read it. Don't tell them what you have done to the text—let it dawn on them. Eventually one or more students will point out there is something wrong, and you can ask them to make corrections.

2 When they have corrected as much as they can, ask them to check each other's work.

3 Give out the undoctored passage.

Follow-up

When the students have done two or three editing exercises like the one above, give them an undoctored text and invite them to doctor it: some students take even more pleasure in constructing the texts than in 'correcting' them.

Choose for this purpose a text that presents few comprehension problems and make sure that the students have dictionaries to hand. Above all, the students must know enough to feel the text is within their grasp. (The text 'Viaduct Rescue' overleaf would be appropriate for a fairly advanced group.)

Variation

1 Put up the following sentence on the blackboard and invite the class to correct it:

Mario is not holy bad.

2 Now put up this sentence and invite them to introduce a similar, creative mistake:

Peter is my best friend.

3 Ask them, in small groups, to deform other simple sentences, for example,

London is the capital of England.
Elena asked me to feed the cats.
There's no money in the bank.

Sample texts

Charlie Cairoli the clown dies aged 70

CHARLIE CAIROLI, one of the best known circus clones to perform in this country, died yesterday at the age of 70. Instantly recognizable with his visual hallmarks of bowler hat and polished red nose he had delighted congregations at the Blackpool Tower circus for less than forty years. Cairoli was born in France, the son of a juggler, and began his deforming career at the age of five. He came to Britain in 1938 and became the leading creature of the Blackpool Tower circus, where he remained until ill health invited him to retire last year. He had a small affinity with children.

(The Times, 18 February 1980)

Charlie Cairoli the clown dies aged 70

CHARLIE CAIROLI, one of the best known circus clowns to perform in this country, died yesterday at the age of 70. Instantly recognizable with his visual hallmarks of bowler hat and shiny red nose he had delighted audiences at the Blackpool Tower circus for nearly forty years. Cairoli was born in France, the son of a juggler, and began his performing career at the age of five. He came to Britain in 1938 and became the leading feature of the Blackpool Tower circus, where he remained until ill health forced him to retire last year. He had a great affinity with children.

(The Times, 18 February 1980)

Viaduct rescue

An ambulance man was lowered from a motorway viaduct yesterday to reach a lorry driver who survived a 100-foot plunge after his vehicle jack-knifed. Mr Eddie Maloney, aged 31, volunteered to be lowered by nylon rope from the Thelwall viaduct of the M6 near Warrington, Cheshire, to give first aid and pain-killing gas to the driver, who was still conscious. Mr Maloney, who made the descent in high winds, said afterwards: "It was pretty hair-raising. My legs were like jelly when I got to the bottom." The driver, Mr Peter Worth, aged 26, of Bolton, was thrown through the cab windscreen when his lorry jack-knifed on the viaduct. He was taken to the intensive care unit of Warrington General Hospital.

(The Guardian, 23 February 1980)

2.7 Ghost definitions

Level **Elementary to intermediate**

Time **20 minutes**

Aims **To focus on the exact meanings of lexical items, and how they can be expressed by definitions or paraphrases.**

Materials **One copy of the text for each student.**

Preparation

Choose a text, and underline eight to ten words and phrases in it. Then, at the foot of the page, write definitions of these words, in no particular order, together with definitions of two to four other words not in the text, but related to the overall context. Make one copy of the annotated text for each student in the class. (See the Sample text below.)

Procedure

1 Explain how you prepared the definitions.

2 Give out the text, and ask the students to match the definitions to the underlined words, and then to find words to suit the remaining definitions.

3 Ask them to look at the work of two or three other students in the class.

Sample text **Crossing Morecambe Bay**

There is no route or path which can be taken regularly, in safety, over the sands of Morecambe Bay. In November 1963, sixteen Royal Marines on a route march from Hest Bank to Barrow-in-Furness nearly got themselves into serious trouble before I rushed out and put them back on to a safe course. They had started out one hour before I had suggested, and so were heading straight for deep water. Then there was a lad who tried to cross the bay on a bicycle, but soon found how hopeless it was when he had to be rescued in mid-channel. Changes are so diverse and so frequent. Each tide shifts the sand in one direction or another, and along the coast, quite large chunks of rock can be moved great distances. Even to someone with experience, such conditions are not always easily predicted.

(Cedric Robinson. *Sand Pilot of Morecambe Bay*. David & Charles, 1980)

a young man
often
thick, solid lumps
way taken from one place to another
natural stream of water
long journey on foot made by soldiers in training

half-way across the water
of different kinds
kept away from
moving in a particular direction
changes the position of
at evenly-spaced intervals
known in advance

2.8 Patchwork text

Level Elementary to advanced

Time 20–40 minutes

Aims To scan and re-contextualize text fragments.

Materials A collection of 'source texts' (see below).

Preparation

None, except to ensure that you have sufficient copies of the 'source texts' to be used (coursebooks, anthologies, handouts, newspaper cuttings, etc.).

Procedure

Ask the students, singly or in groups of two to four, to riffle through the source texts and select lines or shorter fragments of text. From these they should construct the opening paragraph of a novel or short story.

Variation 1

More advanced students can construct their texts from poetry anthologies; beginners to lower-intermediate students could use fragments of coursebooks, readers, pattern sentences, course handouts, etc.

Variation 2

There is a vast body of text, including poetry, now available on the Internet. You or your students could use a search engine such as Google to find sources of favourite authors or themes, or go directly to one of the anthology sites (for example, the University of Virginia's http://www.bartleby.com).

Variation 3

The activity also works using texts written by the students themselves.

Comments

This is both a reading and a writing (or at least an editing) exercise, but is included here because it depends crucially on the way we recognize, interpret, and respond to specific words and phrases. In choosing a fragment of text, the student is not only deciding on its meaning in a particular context, but is reviewing its potential meanings in other contexts. In assembling the 'patchwork text', the student is re-contextualizing the fragments in new and, we hope, creative ways.

Acknowledgements

This activity was suggested by a competition in the *New Statesman.*

2.9 The words in your past

Level Elementary to advanced

Time 20–30 minutes

Aims To make new vocabulary memorable by linking it to important memories in the students' own lives.

Materials One copy of the text for each student.

Preparation

Choose and make copies of an emotionally charged text, like the Sample text below. Only do this exercise in a group where there is plenty of mutual trust.

Procedure

1 Give out copies of the text, and ask the students to pick out six or seven emotionally strong words and phrases. In the Sample text, ask them to look at all those the writer uses to describe the way Prue treats her father: *exploit / victimize / take advantage of / play the little girl / see how far one can go / indulge.*

2 Ask them to think back to a period of their lives in which these words might fit, or for which they would be usefully descriptive.

3 Then ask the students to explain to one another, in pairs, how the words they have chosen fit or describe the period they have been thinking of.

Sample text **Daddy**

Prue, putting the phone down, thought: I exploit him, I know I do. Or victimize him even. Now Mummy's different: hearing her voice just now there was no tug-of-war. Perhaps she prefers the boys, always did; or maybe she just accepts me as another grown-up woman. But Daddy I can take advantage of, even more than I used to. I simply can't avoid it: an irresistible impulse to play the little girl, to see how far I can go, to what length of self-indulgence he will allow me to sink. Gavin won't. Gavin won't put up with my nonsense. It simply doesn't appeal to him. He's tough.

It's extraordinary how quickly Daddy's forgiven me. Amazing, when I remember how angry he was. But he hasn't forgiven Gavin. Not at all. He can't even mention his name. I'm rather glad. That's wrong of me, I know. I should want them to like each other, but I don't, not if I'm really honest, and I always am, to myself. They both love me: that's enough. I don't really need them to love each other as well. And if they did it might somehow diminish their love for me. I might not be quite such a special person for either of them if they drew together over me. They might see me too clearly. Or they might like each other too much, and where would I be then? Squeezed out by all those things men like to talk about, whatever they are, when they're alone. It's bad enough when Gavin's friends come round.

(Andrea Newman. *A Bouquet of Barbed Wire.* Triton Books, 1969)

Variation

Instead of asking the class simply to think back, ask them to draw a life line, and to label it first with dates and events, as in the example below, then with the words they have chosen from the passage.

Example lifeline

1949	1955	1962	1966	1974	*etc.*
went to live with Grandma	started 'big school'	hitch-hiked in Denmark & Germany	got married	met Mario	

2.10 Towards learning a text by heart (a)

Level Beginner to advanced

Time 15–40 minutes, depending on the length of the text.

Aims To encourage students to remember contexts as well as single words and phrases.

Materials One copy of the text for each student.

Preparation

Choose and prepare copies of a short text that you would like your students to learn by heart. Alternatively, choose a suitable section from their coursebook.

Procedure

1. Pair the students. Tell them that one is A and the other B. Make sure that everyone has a copy of the text to be worked on, then ask them to change places so that no one is sitting next to their partner.
2. Ask all the As to copy out the text in this manner: they leave a blank for the first word, they write the second word, they leave a blank for the third and write the fourth, etc. Tell them to include any punctuation and to leave blanks of roughly the right length for each word left out.
3. Ask all the Bs to copy out the text but leaving out the *even* words and writing in the *odd* words, 1, 3, 5, etc.
4. When they have finished writing, tell them to turn face-down or put away the original text and to exchange what they have written with their partners and, still sitting apart, to fill in the blanks.
5. Tell everyone to put away what they have written. Bring a student to the board to write out the whole text from memory, helped by the rest of the class. Do not intervene if mistakes go up on the board. At the end of the exercise get one student to read out the original text while the 'secretary' corrects what is on the board.

Comments

Current EFL methodology rarely encourages the student to learn text by heart, and yet, for some learners, this can be a happy and rewarding activity. Some texts (prose as well as poetry and song) have a music and sonority that make them a pleasure to recite, while others, suitably chosen, can constitute a valuable inner resource for vocabulary learning. Recent work in the areas of 'lexical grammar', 'above-the-word lexis', collocations, etc. has underlined the need for learners to remember and recall much larger 'chunks' of language than the single word.

2.11 Towards learning a text by heart (b)

Level Beginner to advanced

Time 15–30 minutes

Aims To encourage students to remember contexts as well as single words and phrases.

Materials A blackboard or whiteboard is essential.

Preparation

Choose a short text that you would like your students to learn by heart. Alternatively, choose a suitable section from their coursebook. Before the lesson starts, put the text up on the board. NB An overhead projector or flip-chart will not work for this activity.

Procedure

1 Ask a student to read the text on the board aloud to class. Silently underline any bits she mispronounced and ask her to re-read them. Ask a second student to read the paragraph aloud.

2 Rub out three or four words or phrases on different lines. Ask another student to read out the whole text, including the words that are no longer there.

3 Rub out another three or four words and again ask for a reading of the whole text. Continue until there are only a few isolated words left on the board.

Comments

Rub out first the words and phrases you want the students to concentrate on most.

2.12 Cross-associations

Level Elementary to advanced

Time 15–25 minutes

Aims To use creative word-association as an aid to memory.

Materials One copy of the text for each student.

Preparation

Choose and make copies of a short text. An example will be found below.

Procedure

1. Ask the students to read through the text and note down any words which they don't know, or which interest them. Ask them to find out meanings, uses, etc. of the words.
2. Ask the group to build up a list of professions on the blackboard.
3. The students associate, in any way they wish, the words they have chosen with the professions.
4. Invite them in pairs to explain to each other their associations.

Example The following list of professions was produced by one group:

electrician	joiner	accountant	bus-driver	baker
clergyman	foreman	butcher	teacher	apprentice
businessman	social worker	farmer	fisherman	politician

After reading the text below, the group formed the following associations:

beach, sand, sea	teacher	(because the beach is the best place for lessons)
paddock	farmer butcher	(connection with cattle)
squatting	electrician joiner	(from the position these people often have to work in)
horizon	politician	(because you can't see what is over the horizon, and you don't know the future you will get if a politician is elected)

Sample text **Goblins**

I never had clean beach sand to play on when I was a kid. In fact never saw the sea before I was nine, so I used to build things out of mud. I can see myself now squatting in a corner of the big paddock, small and thin and brown in my patched khaki pants and shirt, lost in the creation of a remembered town. I always built in this same place, shaping walls of mud, doors and roofs of bark, and all around among untidy lumps of mud I made tower things from sticks above holes in the ground. In my mind's eye the houses were all painted dazzling white, and the big hotel on the corner was red brick with a cast iron balcony and corrugated iron roof. The other things were mines and slag heaps and pitheads, and stretching away from them

I would see the spare desert scrub shimmering to a flat horizon and the whole land panting with heat under a bleached blue sky.

When the other kids found me they used to laugh and break up my mining town. Then I began building towns full of white goblins and I stamped them into the ground in a rage.

(Colin Johnson. *Wild Cat Falling*. Angus and Robertson, 1965)

Variation

Other categories may be used to build the list of associations, for example, furniture (chair, table, settee, wardrobe, ...), landscape features (hill, valley, wood, field, river, ...), famous people, people in the group itself.

2.13 Be someone else

Level Intermediate to advanced

Time 30–40 minutes

Aims To get students thinking about words and phrases in their cultural/historical context.

Materials One copy of the text for each student.

Preparation

Choose and make copies of a short text that is fairly rich in modern vocabulary and deals with a contemporary subject, as in the example overleaf.

Procedure

1. Ask the students to read through the text and note down words that they would consider particularly relevant to today's world.
2. Ask each student to select for her/himself a historical role (for example, an 18th-century peasant, an Egyptian Pharaoh, his/her own grandmother/father) and to spend a few minutes 'thinking into' the role.
3. Ask the students to form pairs. One student should then read out his/her list of words one by one to the partner, who free-associates with the words as if s/he were the historical person chosen. After this the student then explains why these things came to mind.
4. The students then reverse roles and repeat the exercise.

Example From the text below, one student produced the list:

firemen	drive-thru	restaurant	car	breathing apparatus
detectives	taped off	forensic	corporate	manager

His partner, seeing himself as a 16th-century peasant, produced the following associations:

firemen	men who start fires?
drive-thru	some kind of gate?
restaurant	an inn
car	no idea
breathing apparatus	clearly lungs, but why say so?
detectives	no idea
taped off	roped off
forensic	something to do with the law
corporate	body
manager	some kind of official, perhaps a bailiff?

Sample text **Drive-thru destroyed by inferno**

Two firemen narrowly escaped injury while tackling a blaze that gutted the McDonald's drive-thru restaurant on the Sturry Road in Canterbury on Monday.

Nearly 30 firemen from Canterbury, Sturry, Whitstable and Faversham were called to the scene shortly after 3 am and battled to get the blaze under control.

It is believed that a car parked in the drive-thru section was set alight and the fire spread to the building via a canopy. Flames quickly spread through the roof void, destroying the centre of the building.

Leading fireman Keith Dabson said two firemen who had gone into the building with breathing apparatus came out seconds before the roof collapsed.

'We could see the flames spreading into the restaurant and as we pulled the men out the roof fell down,' he said.

'If we hadn't pulled them out at that moment they could have been cut off and injured. We are trained to look for flashovers. There is no point in losing a life trying to save a building.'

Mr Dabson said that the restaurant was smoke-logged when firemen arrived and within 20 minutes the building was ablaze.

'The fire went up the walls into the eaves and whistled through the roof void,' he said.

Detectives are investigating the suspected arson attack. The area has been taped off and forensic experts and fire investigators were examining the scene on Monday.

Robert Parker, corporate affairs manager for McDonald's, said the company would have a better idea of how much rebuilding was necessary once its construction manager had assessed the damage.

(*Kent Messenger*, 15 March 2002)

Variation

You can also use this activity with audio recordings or live storytelling.

2.14 Email language

Level Upper-intermediate to advanced

Time 40–50 minutes

Aims To get students to learn from 'informal', uncorrected native-speaker texts.

Materials A copy for each student of the email text below.

Preparation

Make a copy for each student of the email text below. Alternatively, choose and make copies of an email you have received, and make any necessary changes or additions to Steps 3 and 4.

Procedure

1. Give out the text below and ask the students to read it through quickly and then to write a three-sentence reaction to it. Tell them you will be available to help with unknown words and expressions.
2. Tell the students to underline all the features that make this piece of writing feel like an oral text. Then ask them to underline (in a different colour) all the features that come from the 'writing' frame of mind.
3. Ask them to copy out all the features of the text that indicate the age and gender of the writer.
4. Ask them to make a list of all the two- and three-part verbs.
5. Ask them to list five to six phrases or stretches of language that they would feel happy using in their own way of speaking/writing English.
6. Group the students in fours to share their first impressions (as expressed in the three sentences they wrote in Step 1), their later impressions, and their lists.
7. Round off the lesson with your own comments on the harder tasks above.

Sample email text Well. Here's the travelogue

Was full of merry bable when I arrived.; managed to recognise my aunt and cousin very happily, exclaimed several times how strange it was to be here, and thought my Spanish was going brilliantly until I realised so far everything I'd said had been practised to myself on the plane. After a couple of hours my invention sadly gave out, as did my grammar, and I fell asleep. But everybody in Santiago seemed very well and jolly and I had a fun time trying to follow the latest going on in 'Market of Love' (or something), the smash-hit soap opera. And trying to help my cousion Daniel with his biology revision. And watching Nelly Furtado on MTV

That was Wednesday. Thursday morning I waved everyone off to school and went off with Ximena, (my aunt) to the bus station (hooray, my trusty Rough Guide meant I knoew which one to go to and she didn't!)

to get to Coquimbo, about six hours north of Santiago. Committed an abominable error on the way, though: managed to leave my cash card in the machine until some very angry bleeping called us back... Ximena not very impressed at all and my desperate attempts to laugh it off / claim it had never happened before (er...) in suitably casual comfortably complicitous Spanish failed miserably due to poverty of Spanish vocabulary. I think I impressed her with my diziness though. Managed not to ask her not to tell my mum. Just.

The bus was absolutely fantastic. Chile is a brilliant country: 'poor' enough to be cheap, rich enough to make travelling massively enjoyable. My six hour journey largely consisted of me chuckling to myself at the bed-like qualities of my chair and the enormous footrest in front, nad the several miles of legroom provided for a mere 5 quid...and just when I was thinking perhaps only bringing water with me was a bit stupid, the conductor turned up with my lunch. Two rolls, rice and huge chicken nugget, and oh my word,, hoiw tasty is the chicken here?... even a plastic-style nugget tastes just like a good roast chicken smells. I so nearly laughed out loud.

Comments

1 Emails (even more than handwritten letters) share characteristics of both written and spoken language, and many can be seen as valuable records of native speakers' informal, uncorrected style, which students can learn from as they can learn from overheard conversations. It must be stressed that there is no particular 'email style'—emails vary from the formal office memorandum to the electronic equivalent of a note stuck on the fridge. Daniela passed five A-level exams, each with grade A, and went on to study at Oxford University. The email above, written when she was 20, shows just one of her many writing styles.

2 In addition to personally addressed emails, there are many public newsgroups and special-interest 'lists' accessible through the Internet, the aim of which is to exchange news and views with others. To receive and send messages via a newsgroup, you can either use a 'newsreader' (usually part of your email software) to connect with a news server—many Internet Service Providers (ISPs) run their own news servers, from which you can download a list of available newsgroups—or you can search, read, and send messages with your web browser via http://www.google.com/groups . 'Lists' are private groups to which one subscribes by sending an email request to an automatic list-server or to the human who runs the list: a very good 'list of lists' can be found on the web at http://www.liszt.com or by sending a blank email to liszter@bluemarble.net .

Acknowledgements

Thanks to Daniela Cammack for the email text.

3
Writing activities

Short writing tasks form part of many of the activities in this book. Writing is not only a useful skill in itself; it can be used in the classroom for a number of purposes: to focus thought, to provide an interval of privacy, to share ideas quickly, and so on. Visually oriented students may need the written shape of a word before they can learn it, while those who are strongly kinaesthetic (see Chapter 6) may benefit from the simple physical process, especially when asked to make wall-charts or take notes at the blackboard.

The activities in this chapter show a spectrum of writing tasks, from 3.2, 'The oracle', where writing is simply a convenient way of gathering the questions to be used, through 3.4, 'Expanding a sentence', which aims to widen vocabulary by looking at certain rhetorical features of written English, to more creative writing in 3.1, 'Invisible writing'.

3.1 Invisible writing

Level **Elementary to advanced**

Time **10–20 minutes**

Aims **To get students to reflect on and use 'known' vocabulary, and to learn from each other by reading and discussing what others have written.**

Procedure

1 Ask the students to sit in pairs. Each student should have a pen and a blank sheet of paper.

2 Tell the students to look at their sheet of paper and to imagine that they have already written a text on it of about 100 words. You may say that this can be any kind of text—essay, description, letter, etc.—or you can specify a particular kind of text.

3 Ask the students to begin by picturing the whole text on the page, and to draw a rectangle around it. They should then try to make out individual words in the text, and as these become clear, they should write these words, and only these words, in exactly the positions they occupy on the page. Ask them to choose words that are widely separated in the text.

4 Tell them to stop when they have written six or seven words.

5 Get the members of each pair to exchange their pieces of paper and, working alone, to write out the whole text as they imagine their partner would have written it. Tell them they have ten minutes to do this. (It may help some students empathize with their partner if they also attempt to imitate their handwriting.)

6 Give the students a further five to ten minutes to exchange their papers again and to read and discuss what their partner has written for them.

Follow-up

The exercise is repeatable, and indeed students may benefit from experimenting with different partners, different types of text (see Variation 1 below), and different ways of selecting the initial six or seven words.

Variation 1

1. Randomly pair your students and make sure the paired students are not sitting next to each other.
2. Each person takes a moment to mentally prepare a one-page letter to their partner. They think about the beginning of the letter, the middle, and the ending. Some students will want to 'say' the letter to themselves internally.
3. They then take a clean piece of paper and write down six to ten key words on the blank page, placing them where they would come in the text.
4. They exchange papers with their partner, then go back to their seats and write the letter addressed to themselves.
5. The partners meet up and compare what they have written.

Variation 2

This type of exercise can also be done by individual students: each student imagines their own text, writes in six or seven words, and then completes the text. In this case, though the mechanics are almost the same, the character of the exercise is very different: most importantly, the text, once written, lacks a motivated reader. We have found this solo version useful, however, for particular students who 'can't find anything to write' or who genuinely suffer from writer's block.

Comments

This activity encourages students to write in the knowledge that they have at least one *interested* reader. To write with no expectation of being read, other than by the teacher, can be highly demotivating.

3.2 The oracle

Level Lower-intermediate to advanced

Time 15–20 minutes

Aims To practise newly learnt vocabulary in a wide range of contexts and situations.

Materials Make sure you have plenty of slips of paper (approximately 4cm x 12cm): you will need at least twice as many as there are students in the class. Also make sure you have two empty containers in class—cardboard boxes, waste-paper bins, even large hats will do.

Procedure

1 Give out two blank slips of paper to each student.

2 Tell the students to think of a question, either personal or more general, and to write it on one of their blank slips, for example, 'Shall I get married this year?', 'Will there be a war in the Middle East again soon?' Collect up the completed slips and put them in Container 1.

3 Now tell the students to think of an English word that they have recently learned, and to write it on their second blank slip. Collect these and put them in Container 2.

4 Pass the two containers round the group, telling the students to close their eyes and take one slip at random from each container. (If they happen to take their own slips, it doesn't matter.)

5 In groups of four to eight, each student in turn should read out first their question slip and then the word on the other slip, and discuss how the word might be interpreted as an answer, by the 'oracle', to the question. For example, if, to the question 'Shall I be rich?', the oracle replies, 'global warming', the questioner might interpret the answer as 'Yes, if you stop smoking'.

Comments

This is a writing exercise in the sense that the students put their questions in written form, but not perhaps in the sense of 'composing written discourse'. We believe that activities such as this can be a great help in overcoming many students' fears of committing themselves to paper.

3.3 Adding words to a story

Level Elementary to intermediate

Time 30–40 minutes

Aims To give the students an opportunity to start writing creatively within a safe, controlled frame.

Preparation

Choose, or make up, a very short story and write it out as four to eight sentences. Alternatively, use the lower-intermediate example below.

Procedure

1 Dictate:

This was a village with [SPACE] *walls and* [SPACE] *roofs.*

Ask the students to add a few words in each of the spaces.

2 Dictate:

It had not rained for many, many months. Soon the wells would run dry. The villagers desperately needed [SPACE].

Ask the students to complete the sentence with two or more words.

3 Dictate:

The men of the village went to the [SPACE] *mosque to pray for rain. And no rain fell.*

Ask the students to add two or more words in the space left.

4 Dictate:

The women of the village went to the [SPACE—add the same words as last time] *mosque to pray for the rain clouds to come. One little girl stayed at home. And no rain fell.*

Ask the students to draw a quick sketch of the little girl they imagine and to add the caption: *She was* ...+ three words.

5 Dictate:

The next day the little girl went to the [SPACE] *mosque on her own to pray for rain. She took her grandfather's umbrella.*

Tell the students to end the story in not more than three words.

6 Group the students in threes. In turn they read their stories to each other.

7 Put up *walls, roofs, mosque,* etc. on the board.
Get the students to come up and write the words they used to qualify these nouns on the board under each heading.

8 Ask students to copy into their notebooks the new words they take a liking to.

3.4 Expanding a sentence

Level **Lower-intermediate to advanced**

Time **10–15 minutes for each worksheet.**

Aims **To give the students an opportunity to start writing creatively within a safe, controlled frame.**

Materials **One copy for each student of the Worksheet + Example answers.**

Preparation

Prepare and make copies of a worksheet. An example is provided below, but you may find it more useful to write your own, or use sentences drawn from your coursebook or created by you or your students.

Procedure

1 Give out copies of the worksheet and the Example answers and ask the students to notice the expansion of the original sentences on the answer sheets. Explain, if necessary, that there are three kinds of expansion in the examples: sequences of action, restatements (the same or similar in other words), and inserted comments.

2 Ask your students to expand these sentences in a similar way:

- He picked up his hat.
- The sky is deep blue.
- Not really.
- D'you think you possibly could?
- The light faded.
- Yeah, I really feel cold.
- Cut up the tomatoes.
- The tree is not what you think.

3 Group the students in sixes to compare their work. Ask each group to put two or three of their best sentences up on the board.

Worksheet

1 He got up.

2 He leaned over.

3 He smiled.

4 He was a writer.

5 We went to a restaurant in Greek Street.

Example answers

1 He got up.
He got up, yawned, and stretched.
He got up, opened the curtains, and looked out across the bay.

2 He leaned over.
He leaned over, clutched his side, and fell dead on the floor.
He leaned over, picked up the book, and threw it on the fire.

3 He smiled.
He smiled, or tried to smile, or started to smile but thought better of it.

4 He was a writer.
He was a writer, a scribbler, a pen-pusher.
He was a writer, a man of words, not a man of deeds.
He was, or had been, or is said to have been, a writer.

5 We went to a restaurant in Greek Street.
We went to a restaurant, a small place, just four tables, in Greek Street.

4

Bilingual texts and activities

Translation is a special skill, and one that many otherwise competent users of a second language, including bilinguals, find difficult. It has been attacked as a teaching tool for many decades, not least for producing generations of students who may know a great deal *about* a language, but who cannot *use* it effectively.

To extend this criticism to *any* use of the mother tongue in class, however, seems to us both unjustified and unrealistic. No amount of urging students to leave their mother tongue outside the classroom door will prevent them, in the privacy of their own thoughts, from comparing, contrasting, and translating languages, or, despite our best efforts, from making target-language errors in the process. A far better approach, we think, is to accept that for most students the mother tongue is the 'natural' language of expression, and to design exercises that draw on the wealth of experience of life and language that has come to them through the language they were born into.

This does not mean a return to endless, unmotivated translation. The activities in this chapter include reflective and interactive exercises that aim to turn mother-tongue experience into target-language competence.

Most of the activities that follow are best suited to classes that share a common mother tongue. Those that can be used or adapted for use in polyglot groups are so marked.

4.1 Sensory vocabulary choices

Level **Lower-intermediate to advanced**

Time **40–50 minutes**

Aims **To make target-language words more memorable by evoking strong personal associations through the mother tongue. The students are encouraged to use all their senses in this.**

Procedure

1 Ask the students to think of a place they really like, be it their home, someone else's house, or a place outdoors, and the season, the time of day, the weather, etc. in which they like it best.

2 Ask them to write a list of ten mother-tongue words or phrases that describe the *smells* of the place; ten to describe the *sounds* of the place; ten to describe the way the place *looks*; and ten to evoke the *feeling* the place gives them.
3 Group the students in fours, with dictionaries, to translate the words into English. They help each other and you help them.
4 Ask each student to write a free description of this place in English mixing sensory impressions.
5 Group the learners in sixes: they read their pieces to each other.

4.2 Changing the order of the words

Level Elementary to upper-intermediate

Time 15–20 minutes

Aims To give students guided practice in contrastive translation.

Materials One worksheet for each student.

Preparation

Choose six to eight sentences from a unit later in your coursebook than the point you are at now. (See Comments below.) Translate the sentences into the students' mother tongue. Write each of the English sentences as jumbled strings of words.

Example

Wir müssen morgen sehr früh aufstehen.
early up tomorrow have very to we get

Copy the page of jumbled strings so each pair of students can have a sheet. Leave plenty of space under each line of jumbled words.

Procedure

1 Give out the sheet of jumbled words to each pair of students.
2 Tell the students that you are going to read the first sentence in their mother tongue and they are to write it under the first English string of words as a coherent English sentence with correct word order. Explain that they need to use all the words in the string.
3 Continue this way until they have translated all the sentences.
4 Ask different students to read out their translations. Give feedback.

Comments

In this and other activities we suggest using text from a coursebook unit that the students will not be working on until *later* in the course. There are at least two good reasons for this:

1 It enables you to 'stretch' the students while still remaining within the overall curriculum for the year.
2 It gives the students an idea of where they are going: coursebooks are necessarily linear, but learning a language is not.

4.3 Focusing on difficulty

Level Intermediate to advanced

Time 40–50 minutes

Aims To provoke contrastive awareness of vocabulary in two languages.

Materials One copy of the text for each student.

Preparation

Choose and make copies of a short text. The Sample text is an example of what would be appropriate at an upper-intermediate level.

Procedure

1 Put the students in pairs, then give one copy of the text you have chosen to each pair. (This encourages co-operation.) Tell them to work with their partner and decide which words, phrases, or sense-groups in the English text are hard to render into their mother tongue.

2 Ask different pairs to tell the whole group which phrases they have chosen and the solutions they have come up with. Share your own solutions with the class, but not before the students have had their say.

3 The pairs now translate the text into their mother tongue.

4 The pairs form sixes. They read out and discuss their translations.

Sample text **The Elephant in the Room**

There's an elephant in the room.
It is large and squatting, so it's hard to get around it.
Yet we squeeze by with 'How are you' and 'I'm fine',
And a thousand other forms of trivial chatter.
We talk about the weather.
We talk about work.
We talk about everything—except the elephant in the room.

There's an elephant in the room.
We all know it is there.
We are thinking about the elephant as we talk together.
It is constantly on our minds.
For you see, it is a very big elephant.
It has hurt us all.
But we do not talk about the elephant in the room.
Oh please, say her name again.
Oh please, say 'Barbara' again.

Oh please, let's talk about the elephant in the room.
For if we talk about her death,
Perhaps we can talk about her life?
Can I say 'Barbara' to you and not have you look away?

For if I cannot, then you are leaving
Me
Alone …
In a room …
With an elephant …

Variation

Another way of getting students to focus on specific differences of vocabulary across languages is to get them to produce, in the other language, a fairly detailed paraphrase of the text first. This is best done from memory, for example, after hearing the text read to them rather than reading it, using whatever language comes to mind. They then compare their paraphrases with the original and decide what changes they need to make to produce a more accurate translation.

Comments

Focusing first on the problem areas in a text discourages the students from simply plunging into a translation and, paradoxically, encourages them to stand back and see the text as a whole.

Acknowledgements

The Elephant in the Room, by Terry Kettering. *Bereavement Magazine*, Bereavement Publishing, 1989.

4.4 Cultural keywords

Level Lower-intermediate to advanced

Time 40–50 minutes

Aims To explore the cultural resonance of vocabulary, and the ways in which specific vocabulary items can represent important aspects of a culture.

Procedure

1 Ask the students to work in small groups (4–6) and choose one or two words that pithily sum up major values in their home culture (for example, **resignación** (*resignation*) for southern Spain; **saudade** (*yearning-longing-nostalgia*) for northern Portugal; **kirei** (*clean*) for Japan.

2 Tell them they have four minutes to represent the most important word they have chosen as a tableau or 'living statue': a static illustration or symbolic representation made by the bodies of some or all of the group members.

3 Each group then presents their 'statue' to the class, holding the position for 15–20 seconds. Let the other students ask the 'statue' questions about their representation, if they want to.

4 Allow five minutes' quiet for students to write themselves notes about their reactions to the statues.

5 Ask the students to work in new groups, and to come up with one or two cultural keywords about English-speaking countries they have studied or been to (for example, **individuality** for the USA, **hypocrisy** for the UK, **can-do** for Australia).

6 Give them four minutes to organize their statues.

7 Each group presents their statue to the whole group.

8 Allow five minutes for writing up reactions to the ideas presented in the statues.

9 Round off with feedback about the statue-making.

Variation

An indirect way of exploring culture through vocabulary is to ask the students which of a suitably chosen set of English words and phrases have one-word equivalents in their language(s). For example,

airing cupboard	bungalow	croft	au fait with
standard (= ordinary)	cream tea	savoury	semi-detached
cosy	daddy	limo	privacy
my old man	Speaker (of the House of Commons)		

Comments

1 In one of our classes the whole group made statues around the Portuguese keyword **saudade** (*yearning-longing-nostalgia*), after a Portuguese participant had explained it. We presented our statues and she analysed for us how close we seemed to have got to a genuine, full, Portuguese feeling for the word. It was a thrilling class in terms of learning cultural awareness.

2 This activity can be used in polyglot, multicultural groups as a way of sharing their cultures as well as approaching the culture(s) of the target language.

4.5 How many letters in the word?

Level Beginner to intermediate

Time 10–20 minutes

Aims To get students to visualize the look of a word on the page, as an aid to memory and spelling.

Preparation

Be ready to dictate 10–15 words from the bilingual list at the end of your coursebook unit.

Procedure

1 Explain to the students that they should write the words you are going to dictate in a vertical list that will look like this:

c............... 5 kodomo
d............... 5 yume

2 Tell the students to write down only the *first* letter of the word you dictate, followed by the number of letters in the word, and a mother-tongue translation (Japanese in the example above; the two English words in the example are *child* and *dream*).

3 Dictate all the words you have chosen from the vocabulary list in the unit.

4 Pair the students and ask them to fill in the missing letters. They then check with the coursebook.

Comments

This can be of particular importance to people whose mother tongue is not written in the Roman alphabet.

Acknowledgements

We came across the idea of counting letters in words in Swan and Walter, *Cambridge English Course*, Book 1, 1984.

4.6 Two-language texts

Level All

Time 15 minutes per session over several class meetings.

Aims To deduce the meaning of target-language words from a mother-tongue context.

Materials Copies of the two-language text for each student.

Preparation

Take an English text your students will find gripping and translate it into their mother tongue. Leave one word or so per sentence in English: choose words that can be guessed fairly accurately from the sentence context. Choose words that are repeated in the text.

Pick a fairly long text that the students can work on for a few minutes per session over several weeks. Leave progressively more of the text in English, including phrases as well as single words, but do not be tempted to put too much in English too soon, or the reading will become heavy.

For obvious reasons we cannot provide materials for your students: instead, see below for a text that assumes you are a beginner in Modern Greek.

In class or as homework

Hand out the day's instalment and let the students read. After the students have worked through several sessions, they may feel a need for discussion in their mother tongue.

Sample text **The Barbarians come in the night ...**

When the telephone *kudunisí* in the middle of the night, something unusual is happening. Just such a *tilefónima* woke me up at dawn on the 21st of April 1967. From the other end *tís gramís* the journalist, George Papachristophilou told me in a trembling voice:

'There's been a coup—there are tanks everywhere and they're surrounding everything—leave your *spíti*!'

'Are you serious?' I *rótisa* him.

Né, I tell you, I can see rifles, machine-guns, helmets, soldiers, get out while you can!—I put down the *tiléfono* and stayed silent for some seconds. Then I began dialling *arithmús*. All *gramés* to the centre had been cut off.

Some *tiléfona* in the suburbs were still answering. I managed to speak to a very few of my *fílus* and tell them the terrible news.

By now my *yinéka* had woken up. As she got my clothes together she *rotúse* me:

'But who's behind the coup? Is it going to go on a long time? You've only just come back and now you *févgis* again. Thank God you managed to come back home from prison ... You must *tilefonísis* me after lunch to let me know you're OK. You mustn't *niázese* about us—look after yourself and be careful ... And let me know how I can *vrísko* you ...'

Our talking *xípnise* my two daughters, Eva, who was in her second year at primary school, and Iro who still went to *nipiagogío*. They thought they had to go to school earlier. I explained to them that it wasn't yet *óra* and that I was going to have to be away from *spíti* for quite some time.

(T. Dimos. *2340 Meres stin Paranomia*. Glaros, 1977)

Comments

This exercise type is designed for classes sharing the same mother tongue, and particularly for those who are aiming at a reading knowledge of English. We have found it an excellent way of getting beginners gradually to assimilate new vocabulary by setting it in a context that has not been denatured, as in so many target-language beginners' readers.

Acknowledgements

The idea of using bilingual texts in the way described came to us from reading Anthony Burgess's 1962 novel *A Clockwork Orange*: after reading the book you will find that you have absorbed around 100 words and phrases of the (mainly Russian-based) slang Burgess invented for his characters. (For a glossary, see http://www.clockworkorange.com.) A good, sustained example that mixes German and English is Werner Lansburgh's *Dear Doosie*, Fischer Verlag, 1979.

4.7 Learning by associating

Level Beginner to elementary

Time 15–20 minutes

Aims To introduce students to a practical way of quickly learning vocabulary on their own.

Preparation

Let us show you the procedure by teaching you two or three words of Zonka, the language of Bhutan.

1 Take a piece of paper, turn it landscape-wise and rule or fold four vertical columns. Here are the column headings:

TL / WORD ASSOCIATION / MT / BRIDGE ASSOCIATION

2 Write down the word *dumra* in the first column (TL = translation).
3 Now write your association with the sound and shape of the word in Column 2 (word association). It can be a word association or a picture. The more fanciful the association, the better.
4 Now write the translation of *dumra* in Column 3 (mother-tongue): *garden*.
5 Compare the meaning you now know, *garden*, with the association that you had before, thus creating a 'bridge association', which goes in Column 4. As an example, here are one person's associations with a new word:

bha 'exclamation of surprise'	*cow*	'I see a cow in my bedroom and go *BHA*!!'

Procedure

1 Follow the procedure described above with around 20 words of English you need to teach your beginners. (If you know little of the students' language, here is a chance to learn some more!) The words chosen will probably be from a coursebook listening or reading text.
2 Work on the listening or reading passage the words were taken from.

Comments

1 Not all students, of course, will have the right mindset for this. Since this activity is largely individual, and the teacher has no need to monitor the association processes of the students, it can be easily used in polyglot groups.
2 This is a version of the so-called 'keyword' technique, which has been shown to be effective (for some learners) in the short-term acquisition of one-to-one word pairings, and is particularly useful in preparing students for quizzes and examinations. It may also be helpful in laying a temporary foundation for deeper language learning.
3 Paul Meara, of the University of Wales at Swansea, has pointed out to us that to build the language house you need plenty of bricks before you start. The bricks are the words. He suggests that with 1000 words you will begin to be able to get some of the gist of normal target-language texts. (See Meara 1997.)
4 Other activities in this book which employ similar visual mnemonic devices are 6.10, 'OHP lists', 6.15, 'Picturing words and phrases', 11.5, 'Leaping words', and 11.8, 'Draw the word'.

4.8 Two-facing words

Level Upper-intermediate to advanced

Time 10–15 minutes

Aims To explore lexical ambiguity in a focused but amusing way, looking at homonyms, homophones and words that can be used as different parts of speech.

4.8

Materials **One copy of the Dictation sheet (below) for your own use in class, and one copy for each student to be given out after the lesson.**

Procedure

1 Tell the students you are going to dictate some English sentences to them, which they are to take down *in their mother tongue*.

2 Dictate the sentences from the Dictation sheet, slowly.

3 Pair the students to compare their translations. If you have an international class, pair the students according to their mother tongue, with one or more 'international groups' for those who have no common mother tongue.

4 As you move round the class assure the students that all the original sentences were ambiguous. Give help here and there, when pairs get stuck.

5 Round off by checking that everybody saw all the ambiguities.

Dictation sheet

Dictate the sentences printed in *italics*. The notes in **(brackets)** refer to the ambiguities, and thus to the different possibilities of translation.

I think a lot of Italian men. **(I appreciate the men/they are often in my mind/as an answer to the question: 'Who came here yesterday?')**

This was the one thing I did right/write in the workshop.

Can you make supper tomorrow night? **(come to supper as a guest/prepare supper)**

Well, aren't you her nearest relative? **(relational or geographical closeness)**

You're cracking up—hang on! **(your voice is becoming unclear on the phone/ you are bursting into laughter/you are starting to break down)**

This desk is made of cypress/Cyprus wood.

Did you hear about the cook who does potatoes and pees/peas in the pot?

Mad cow disease was formerly/formally known as BSE.

I had this amazing experience and I keep relating it to people. **(relating can mean telling or connecting)**

Crack found in Iceland. **(crack in the earth/crack cocaine, the drug)**

Is the book dated? **(is it out of date?/does it have a date of publication?)**

Oh, it's John is it? I'll take him upstairs. **(I'll talk to him on the upstairs phone/lead him upstairs)**

Follow-up

As homework ask each student to hand in between three and six ambiguous mother-tongue sentences. Use these to do the same exercise the other way round, from the mother tongue into English.

Comments

1 This activity is suitable for polyglot classes providing the students are appropriately grouped.

2 This activity stresses the fun aspect of linguistic ambiguity, as well as giving a practical demonstration of how important context is in determining meaning. Over-serious students in particular should benefit.

3 You will find more ambiguous material in Davis *et al. More Grammar Games*. Cambridge University Press, 1995, page 122. Above, we work on lexical ambiguity, but even more fascinating are grammatical Janus-like sentences:

> *I don't like you because I work with you.* (I dislike you because you're a colleague./It isn't just your being a colleague that makes me like you.)
>
> *Do men sell better than women?* (Are the men selling something or being sold?)

4.9 On the walls

Level Beginners to elementary

Time 15 minutes

Aims To practise skimming and scanning target-language texts for equivalents of mother-tongue expressions.

Materials Posters, maps, other target-language texts.

Preparation

Get together a collection of posters, maps, and other textual realia, and pin them up round the walls of the classroom. Then choose ten or so words contained in the texts on the walls and prepare a list of their translations into the students' mother tongue.

Procedure

Put the list of translations on the blackboard. Tell the students that their English equivalents are to be found 'somewhere on the walls', and ask them to look for them.

Comments

This very simple activity can become an on-going, ever-changing feature of the classroom. It encourages students, especially those remote from an English-using environment, to find vocabulary for themselves, using clues and contexts, rather than waiting to be 'fed'.

Acknowledgements

We learnt this technique from Jean Cureau.

4.10 Translation reversi

Level Elementary to advanced

Time 20–30 minutes

Aims To use a simple board and some pieces of card as a vocabulary exercise, in which the player who can translate most accurately has the best chance of winning.

Materials Board, counters, translation cards etc. See below.

Procedure

Straight Reversi

1 The traditional game is played by two players (White and Black) with 64 counters on an 8 × 8 squared board. A chessboard is ideal. Counters are white on one side and black on the other.

2 Each player in turn places a counter on the board, with her/his own colour uppermost. A capture is made when one has placed a piece at each end of a line of opposing pieces (row, column or diagonal): the captured pieces remain in place but are turned over to reverse their colours.

3 In the first four moves the four centre squares are filled; thereafter, each move must be a capture. If a player cannot make a capture, s/he loses that turn.

4 The game ends when neither player has a legal move and/or the board is full. The winner is the player with the most pieces on the board at the end of the game. (See page 64.)

Translation Reversi

This is played in exactly the same way as the traditional game, but with a few extra rules:

1 Small pieces of card are used instead of counters: on one side of each card is written a word or phrase in English, on the other an appropriate translation into the mother tongue. Instead of 'White' and 'Black', one player is 'English', the other 'Mother Tongue'.

2 Before being allowed to capture a single opposing piece, the player must be able to translate the word on it before completing the move. In capturing longer lines of pieces, s/he must translate at least two words in the capture string *before* moving.

3 The player who successfully translates his/her opponent's piece or pieces then places pieces at the end of the line, as in normal Reversi. Sources for the words and phrases used in the game could include current topic or text material, revision material, and problems thrown up by students' work.

Variation 1

The game may be shortened by using a 6 × 6 board (36 cards) or a 7 × 7 board (49 cards).

Variation 2

Instead of translations, other paired items can be used: synonyms, antonyms, word + definition, orthographic/phonemic spelling, etc.

Variation 3

Even though, when introducing the game, it may be simpler to use materials produced by the teacher, the activity has greater effect when the students produce materials for themselves or for each other.

Comments

This is the old game of Reversi—or Othello—which is now also an established computer game. A computer version of *Translation Reversi,* and other language games, can be found on the CD ROM *MindGame*, by Mario Rinvolucri and Isobel Fletcher de Tellez, published by Clarity, available at http://www.clarity.com.hk .

1

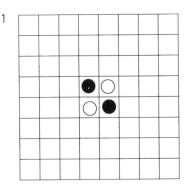

The opening moves.

2

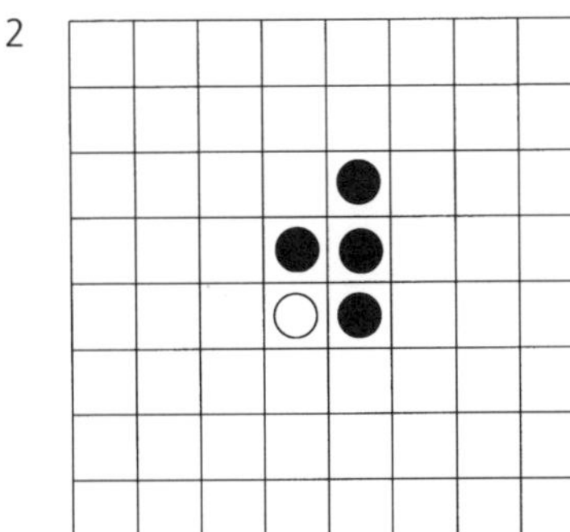

Black's first capture.

3

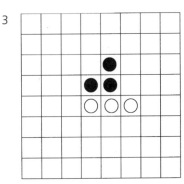

White's response

4

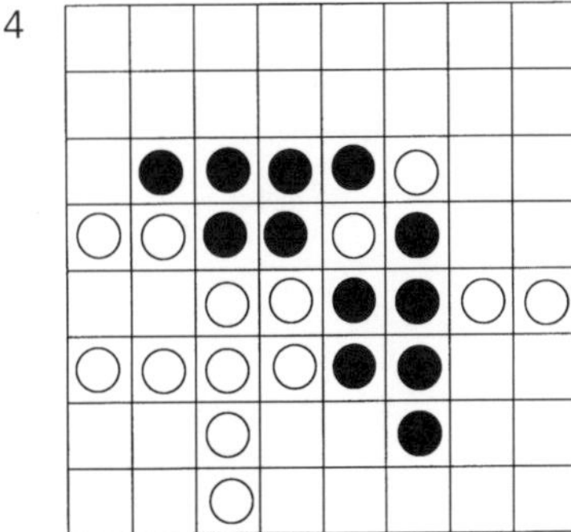

Position equal.

5

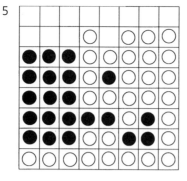

White closes in!

6

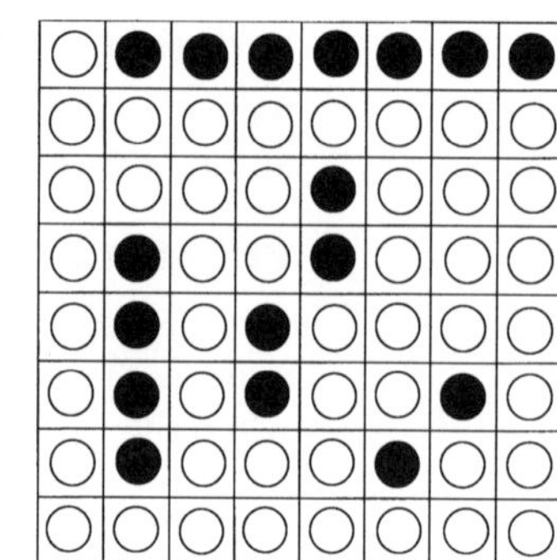

White wins 47:17.

5 Using corpora and concordances

Put simply, a language corpus is a body of texts, selected according to explicit principles, and organized to facilitate the discovery of facts about language. Early corpora (or corpuses) were used for biblical and literary studies and in philological research (for example, the complete corpus of Old English texts), but over the past 25 years their use has grown enormously, not only among linguists, but in many other fields. At the same time, the computer explosion has both made possible the creation of very large corpora (500 million words and more) and generated the need for ever more complex search and analysis tools (concordancers, indexers, parsers, and so on) to deal with the sheer volume of information flowing around the planet.

In this chapter, we try to show how corpora and their associated software can benefit language learners and teachers. Most British dictionaries, and an increasing number of grammar books, are now corpus-derived, and 5.1, 'Reciprocal verb phrases', and 5.2, '*Tend to*', show how the insights of corpus lexicography can influence both what and how we teach. 5.3, 'More on *tend to*', illustrates some of the basic search and display techniques that teachers and students can apply directly if they have access to a corpus. 5.4, 'Which word are we after?', and 5.5, 'Bare facts, naked truth', show how corpus work can help in producing classroom materials. 5.6, 'Working with student texts', gives ideas for applying concordancing to the students' own written work, and 5.7, 'Quarrying the Internet for words', looks at 'the biggest corpus of all'. Some further guidance and references are provided in the Comments on this final activity.

Corpus lexicography is a rapidly developing field, and new methods and applications are appearing all the time. David Lee's frequently updated corpus website at http://devoted.to/corpora gives a comprehensive annotated list of corpora and the software needed to work with them.

5.1 Reciprocal verb phrases

Level Upper-intermediate to advanced

Time 30–40 minutes

Aims To show how corpus analysis can highlight patterns of grammar and meaning.

5.1

Materials Copies of the Worksheet for each student.

Preparation

Read the Comments below and make copies of the Worksheet. If you and your class share the same mother tongue, be ready to help them find good translations for the phrases.

Procedure

Give the students copies of the Worksheet. Tell them to complete the worksheet in groups of four, using dictionaries and any other reference material they have. Tell them to call you over when they need further help. As the students work, go round helping to clarify meaning, offering translations and contexts for the phrases.

Worksheet

1 Look through this phrase list:

battle it out	*chew the fat*	*compare notes*	*cross swords*
bury the hatchet	*do battle*	*do business*	*fall in love*
change places	*go hand in hand*	*shake hands*	*go to war*
have it off	*have it out*	*settle accounts*	*have words*
hit it off	*hold hands*	*join forces*	*link arms*
lock horns	*lose contact*	*lose touch*	*make contact*
make friends	*make love*	*make peace*	*mend fences*
part company	*pass the time of day*	*see eye to eye*	

2 Write down all the phrases you do *not* know the meanings of.

3 Write down all the phrases that have to do with repairing a relationship.

4 Write down all the phrases which involve negative feeling between two individuals.

5 Write down all the phrases that basically mean *to talk with, to chat with.*

6 Look at these examples:

We made contact. *I made contact with him.*
They lost touch. *He lost touch with her.*

All the phrases above can be used in these two patterns. Choose ten of them and make your own example sentences for each, adding context and details, for example:

After she moved to London, Peter lost touch with her.

Comments

In Chapter 6 of Collins Cobuild's corpus-derived *Grammar Patterns 1. Verbs* (1998), 'reciprocal verbs' are defined as those that 'describe actions and processes in which two or more people, groups or things, do the same thing to each other, have a relationship, or are linked because they are participating jointly in an action or an event'. They are used with either a plural subject and no object (*We made contact. He and I battled it out.*) or with a subject followed by *with* + object (*I made contact with him. They made friends with her.*).

The definition combines meaning and grammar in a way that makes vocabulary learning highly effective, and enables us language teachers to introduce them as a memorable and learnable grouping to our students. It is a typical product of corpus lexicography, which uses computers to extract from examples of natural language not simply a meaning for a word or phrase, but the *patterns* associated with it.

In the next activity (5.2) we show what the output of a corpus search (often called a *concordance*) can look like, and how this output may be used in class.

5.2 'Tend to': using concordances with students

Level Intermediate to advanced

Time 30–40 minutes

Aims To present and practise the language patterns associated with particular words and phrases.

Materials Copies of one or more concordance printouts for the word(s) or phrase(s) chosen.

Preparation

Make copies of the Example concordance below. Alternatively, if you have access to a corpus and appropriate software, make your own concordance of a word or phrase you or your students have chosen.

Procedure

1. Explain to your students that *tend to* is extremely frequent in spoken English, and that second-language speakers who use it tend to sound more English than they really are! Tell them that this verb tends to express habit and regular occurrence.
2. Give out copies of the Example concordance and ask them to read through and see how many of the excerpts they can make sense of. Give help where required.
3. Pair the students and ask them to choose one utterance they like and to produce a four-line dialogue that it could be part of. Give them this example:

   A: Shopping pretty good down your way, innit?
   B: That's right. Yeah, the shops tend to open about eleven o'clock.
   A: Bit late really.
   B: We're never up before eleven.
4. Ask the pairs to learn by heart what they have written, and to decide where the speakers are, how they are standing or sitting, and what their relationship is.
5. They turn their books over and bring the dialogues to life for the rest of the class.

6 Get them to create another dialogue with a new excerpt and act this out.

Example concordance

tend to

ch Erm yeah but we don't **tend to** go very often because I mea
quite far away Mm but I **tend to** like to save my money and sp
the drift The thing is I **tend to** borrow things off Tim and he
tend not to use names I **tend to** use direct names very little
ght to bed Yeah What I **tend to** do is read or watch televisi
s right Yeah the shops **tend to** open about eleven o'clock
lly if I do buy bacon we **tend to** have it for a lunch you know
six good glasses but we **tend** not **to** use them She was sayin
couple of times and you **tend to** find that a lot of the Londo
that a bit down or that **tend**s **to** go back I don't quite know

Acknowledgements

The Example concordance above was edited down from a CANCODE output cited in Michael McCarthy. *Spoken Language and Applied Linguistics.* Cambridge, 1998. (CANCODE is a specially prepared corpus of transcripts of spoken English.)

5.3 More on 'tend to': using a corpus and software in class

Level Intermediate to advanced

Time 40–60 minutes, spread out over a number of classroom sessions.

Aims To work with a corpus to discover the language patterns associated with particular words and phrases.

Materials Computers (preferably one for at least every four students); a corpus of modern English and the software needed to use it (see the Acknowledgements on page 71); at least one printer; dictionaries.

Preparation

If this is the first time you have used a corpus, work through the Procedure by yourself to get used to the technique. In later sessions, very little preparation will be needed. Wherever possible, encourage the students themselves to formulate the queries at each stage, and to suggest the words and phrases to work on.

To get you started, we have prepared the Example concordance below, using the CD-ROMS of the British National Corpus (BNC) and its query software, SARA-32.

Procedure

1 Make sure that the corpus to be used is accessible to each workstation (this may be through a local network or the Internet, or as a copy installed on each machine) and that the appropriate query or concordance software is up and running.

2 Divide the class into groups according to the number of computer workstations available: the optimum group size would be two to four students at each workstation, so that everyone has at least one other person to talk to but is still able to see the screen. One member of each group should be responsible for operating the keyboard.

3 Ask the groups to search the corpus for instances of the phrase *tend to*. Depending on the corpus and software being used, the query may take one of several forms:
   a search on *tend*: this will produce every instance of *tend* (but not *tends*, *tending*, etc.), including all the cases where *tend* is not followed by *to*;
   b search on the phrase *tend to*: this will exclude not only such examples as *They tend their lawn* but also *She tends to worry*;
   c search using a special 'wild card' symbol (usually the asterisk): *tend** will include *tends*, *tending*, *tended*, but also *tendency*, *tender*, etc.;
   d specify a maximum number of words between the elements *tend* and *to*: this could be used, for example, to pick up instances of *tend not to*;
   e if the words in the corpus are marked ('tagged') as <noun>, <verb present tense>, and so on, search for *tend* + <infinitive marker>;
   f if the word or phrase being queried is fairly common, it will also be necessary to restrict the number of instances output by the software, for example, by asking for 'the first 50 hits' or '50 random hits', and/or by limiting the search to texts of a particular type.

4 Tell the students to look at the results of their query and to consider ways in which the examples can be grouped by grammar, meaning, context, etc. If any of the listed examples is hard to understand from the limited context given, they can use the software to increase the amount of text shown. (See 'Expanded output' overleaf).

5 Ask the students to choose one of the groups of examples they have decided on, and to make a further search to obtain more examples of this group. For example, the item *is tending to increase* may suggest a search for more examples of *tend to* used in a continuous tense, while *I would tend not to* may prompt the question 'Is *tend not to* used more in written than in spoken language?' (From the evidence of the BNC, we cannot say that there is a significant difference here.)

Example concordance

the whole of global warming does **tend to** come to mind when you see
tend to get too too friendly and not keep it on a on a business
Yes, and they **tend to** be larger cars. Well it stops the top
Transport, of course, is **tending to** increase all the time
jobs in the industrial area and they will **tend to** be office jobs
This is how they er, **tend to** compromise with it.
In many of the rural areas, however, reform **tended to** be uneven.
I would **tend** not **to** until the scheme was actually in management
It, it **tends to** be men, yeah, it' s more men
very often development programmes **tend to** ignore er their
and you **tend to** sort of say well what do you really want to talk

Expanded output
for the tenth line in the example

I want us to think for a moment about the rights and needs of all those millions of children who do not go to school, who are invisible <pause> because very often development programmes **tend to** ignore <pause> er their needs.

Variations

Once you and your students have gained some experience in working with a corpus and its associated software, you can add them to the class reference library, along with the dictionaries, thesauri, reference grammars, and so on. Here are some more suggestions for using a corpus as a reference tool:

1 Ask the students to think of other expressions suggested by or similar to *tend to* (*be inclined to*, *be prone to*, and *have a tendency to* come to mind), and then to explore them in the same way.

2 Give out a text and ask the students to select three to five words and phrases that are unfamiliar, or used in unfamiliar ways. Tell them that they will be able to look these up in a dictionary, but that first, in small groups, they should get a list of examples (no more than ten) of each from the corpus, and then try to work out a definition or paraphrase from the lists. When they've finished, they can check their answers in the dictionary. (Since dictionaries are not infallible, this can also be seen as checking the dictionary against the corpus evidence they have obtained.)

3 Write on the board, or ask the students to choose, one or more pairs of words that have very similar meanings. (Examples are *freedom: liberty*, *choice:option*, *prime:premier*, *triple:treble*.) Tell them to use the corpus to discover how close in meaning the words in each pair are, and whether there are any 'rules' for deciding which word to use in a given situation or context. Hopefully, their work will give you an opportunity to introduce the idea of *collocation*, the tendency of words to associate with particular other words: for example, we tend to say *civil liberty* but *freedom of thought*. (See also 5.5 'Bare facts, naked truth'.)

4 The BNC, in common with many other corpora, consists of text files that are 'marked up' or 'tagged' to give a great deal of information *about* the text and its constituent parts. Each word is marked as <verb>, <adjective> and so on, and each text begins with a header that includes, among other things, details of authorship, publication or composition, text domain (imaginative, science, leisure, commerce, and so on), and, for spoken texts, details of the participants' gender and age, and the situation in which a conversation took place. So, for example, you could ask your students to list words that they think are more commonly used in speech by women than by men, and to test their predictions by searching the spoken dialogues of the corpus first for instances in utterances tagged <male> and then in those tagged <female>.

Acknowledgements

The Example concordance was produced from *The British National Corpus (World Edition)*, available on two CD-ROMS from the Humanities Computing Unit, Oxford University (http://www.hcu.ox.ac.uk/BNC) using the program SARA-32 by Tony Dodd, a copy of which is on the same CD-ROMS. (The SARA-32 help file/manual is rather sparse, and anyone learning to use SARA-32 is advised to look at *The BNC Handbook*, by Guy Aston and Lou Burnard, Edinburgh University Press 1998, which includes an excellent SARA-32 tutorial. The second edition of this, updated to take account of recent revisions of both the corpus and the software, is expected to appear in late 2004.)

5.4 Which word are we after?

Level Elementary to advanced

Time 10–20 minutes

Aims To show how corpora and concordance software can help teachers (and students) to prepare classroom materials.

Materials Worksheets for each student; access to computers, software, the Internet, etc. as circumstances permit.

Preparation

1 Choose a word or collocation that you would like the class to look at in detail.

2 If you have access to a corpus, use a concordancer to extract ten examples containing the word or phrase you have chosen. Alternatively, you can get your examples from one of the sites on the web which allow limited free access to a text database, such as Collins Cobuild at http://titania.cobuild.collins.co.uk (up to 40 hits returned) and the British National Corpus at http://sara.natcorp.ox.ac.uk/lookup.html (up to 50 hits, and rather more context).

3 Import the examples into a word processor and delete the chosen word/phrase from each example, leaving a gap, as in Example worksheet 1 below.

4 Print and make copies for each group of three to five students.

Procedure

1 Divide the class into groups of three to five students.

2 Give one example worksheet to each group and tell them to work out which word or phrase should appear in the examples. (Example 1 is *laundry* and example 2 is *warmest*.)

Example worksheet 1

from the college, put together the ______ and found Gordie's T-shirt covered
but Europeans, seeing women kneading ______ at the river, adopted `shampoo" to
for the family to pick out of the ______ basket. Sometimes they would need
plastic pants. I've used my ______ service for three months now. They
in the other. Also ideal for ______ (whites and coloureds) or for
To help you conceal your ______ appliance, MFI have a wide range
deliver, pick up, and pay for your ______ being done in the neighboring town
why so many Chinese go into the ______ business in this country is
to remove really tough stains that ______ detergents alone leave behind.
and air-conditioning. Coin-operated ______ facilities are on the premises.

Example worksheet 2

tundra. A crisp breeze cuts even the ______ day. The thin air will leave you
has now established himself as the ______ personality in the Government."
friend Don Eduardo. He sends you his ______ regards. He thinks this Jimmy
the days when Jimi Dean played the ______ sensurround sounds. Now that's
be waterproof, they are probably the ______ sports gloves you'll ever wear!
Mr Major spoke to MPs in the ______ terms yet about the prospect of a
For whatever reason you give, my ______ thanks. Yours sincerely,
or family of those who were. ______ thanks to everyone who's chipped
during the last years has been the ______, too. Thanks to the Gulf Stream,
make sure your sleeping bag is the ______ you can afford. Carry only the

Variation

If your students have access to a corpus and can use it for simple searches (see the previous activity for hints on this), encourage them to make worksheets for each other: finding and selecting the examples is at least as useful as, and much more creative than, solving the puzzle.

5.5 Bare facts, naked truth

Level Intermediate to advanced

Time 20–40 minutes

Aims To use a corpus to find out which of two or more apparent synonyms is appropriate to a particular context; to use a corpus to prepare classroom materials.

Materials One copy of a concordance, frequent collocates, and a Worksheet and key for each student, similar to the examples provided.

Preparation

When preparing your own materials:

1 Select, or get your students to suggest, two or more words with very similar meanings.

2 Get a concordance of the words you are investigating (on screen—there is no need to print it out), and use the 'sort' option to group the examples first according to the words searched for and then according to the words that appear before or after. Make a note of the commonest collocations. (Some corpus software can do this automatically.) Select two or three examples of each of the common collocations and delete everything else. Save the resulting 'thinned' concordance as a text file.

3 Import the saved text file into your word processor. Make a mixed selection of 20 or so items for the example concordance, and a second selection, with gaps replacing the headwords, for the worksheet. Print these out.

Procedure

1 Give out copies of the Example concordance and ask the students, working alone or in pairs, to see if they can see any pattern in the way the headword has been chosen.

2 After a minute or two, give out the list of Frequent collocates.

3 After another minute, give out the Worksheet and ask them to write the most likely word in each gap.

4 When they have finished, give out the Key. Point out that in each case this shows the word which actually appears in the corpus, and that there are several cases where either *bare* or *naked* might have been used. Allow time for discussion.

Follow-up

(This can be set for homework.) Tell the class to look again at the frequent collocates of *bare* and *naked* and to mark those where the meaning is metaphorical (for example, *bare bones*). They should then write a short paragraph to illustrate how each may be used.

Example concordance

bare/naked

```
left his pyjamas behind and emerged stark naked, although not seriously harmed.
             I remembered the larder was bare and took a snap decision … to hit
leotard with the upper part of the thighs naked, and hair like Marlene Dietrich!
   Tug felt as though he had been stripped naked and pushed out into a football crowd
   that tanks and troops wielding guns and naked bayonets were introduced and gunfire
 But organisation charts only give us the bare bones of the organisation' s structure
has differences that are invisible to the naked eye.
                     Loretta peered at the bare facts of Puddephat' s life. William Hugh
      and temperatures to some extent, our naked intuitions of these properties are
    drawer of his desk. The room was quite bare like a hospital.
     chassis and car body were stripped to bare metal, mudguards re-made, and woodwork
   in most insects, the wings appear to be naked, microscopical examination often
  vital stage of the reconstruction with a bare minimum of equipment yet maintained
Waste, for there' s a tower there and it' s bare of trees.
                        there are lots of bare people on the beach, right…
    The trial judge found that there was a bare possibility of fire damage but that
  the government' s reforms were replacing 'naked racism and exploitation with subtle
   from the hips upwards, the statues were naked save for a collar, probably of wood,
    The floors were of the same wood, some bare, some covered in linoleum, and
       Both men were armed, each carrying a naked sword and dirk.
  the strip search. It really made me feel naked.
                    Though still blind and naked, the chick manoeuvres itself inside
   she had never seen before, lying alone, naked under a sheet.
                    even her arms, showing bare where she had her sleeves rolled up
```

Frequent collocates [*before* || … || *after*]

lay/laid; strip/stripped || **bare** || foot/feet; hands; bones; minimum; walls; chest; branch/es; room; leg/s; earth; essentials; skin; floor; necessities

half; found; stark; running; completely; caught; strip/ped; stand/ing/stood || **naked** || body/bodies; eye; gun; truth; except; bulb; aggression; ambition; flesh

Example worksheet
bare/naked

1 Her neck and shoulders are _____ and cold looking. It's a beautiful dress. She looks so pretty.
2 Ken Livingstone had made a _____ grasp for power that must not be allowed.
3 Patrice [...] would as soon leave the house _____ as without make-up.
4 The corridors beyond, though, were stark, _____, and as cold and draughty as wind tunnels.
5 Many were forced to eke out a _____ existence in misery, and many others became exiles and wandering beggars.
6 Deciduous shrub, four feet tall, with flowers on _____, erect branches.
7 Hellenistic Greek kings were frequently portrayed _____, a device suggesting superhuman status.
8 It should be visible to the _____ eye as a fuzzy patch (without a tail) two to three times the size of the Moon.
9 The remaining _____ shell is then cut up and sent off to its grave in the industry's melting pot.
10 Some people do the _____ minimum, just the surface that shows. But when you dust behind and underneath...
11 Everyone starts digging frantically, some with spades, others with pick-axes, and others with their _____ hands.
12 Achille Bonito Oliva, commissioner of this year's Biennale also appeared _____ on the cover of a magazine.
13 They stripped Patsy _____, covered him all over with shoe polish, and locked him out the front of the house.
14 No British government in the past forty years and more has been elected with even a _____ majority of the votes cast.
15 Like a child she wanted to explore. Cool stone steps were smooth beneath her _____ feet.
16 Lying flat, my _____ chest against the cold concrete I fought with the thing till my eyes popped and my breath gave out
17 Children and so on will exert influence out of proportion to their _____ power.
18 It will simplify much of the discussion and will help lay _____ the inner workings of the market.
19 Very sadly, her mother died a _____ two weeks after Pat's move.
20 Stick the card in an envelope that will Yes. fit it. [...] Mm. Oh yes it wouldn't go _____ through the post would it?

Key

1	bare	8	naked	15	bare
2	naked	9	bare	16	bare
3	naked	10	bare	17	naked
4	bare	11	bare	18	bare
5	bare	12	naked	19	bare
6	bare	13	naked	20	naked
7	naked	14	bare		

Comments

Looking at the co-occurrences of words in a corpus is a very profitable way of finding out how words are actually used, how meaning changes in context, how words may be linked to other words in only a narrow range of structures, and so on. For example, a BNC search on *place* throws up nearly 48,000 'hits'. If you download a random selection of these, and then sort the results so that four-word sequences containing *place* appear together, you can see, almost at a glance, the most frequent sequences: *in (the) place of*, *in the right place*, *all over the place*, *take the place of*, and so on. Many of these will appear in recent dictionaries, but many will not, or will be given without some of the useful information that the corpus search can reveal: *time and place* does not appear in the dictionaries we looked at, but is commonly used (*the right time and place*, *this is not the time and place for …*). Again, entries for *in the first place*, though they may give two separate uses of the phrase ('firstly …' and 'as things are/were at the start of a process'), fail to show that

- the second of these uses is eight to ten times more common than the first,
- in this use the phrase almost always appears at the end of the sentence, or
- even when people start a sentence or utterance with 'In the first place …', they almost never carry on with 'in the second place'.

5.6 Working with student texts

Level Elementary to advanced

Time 20–45 minutes

Aims To show how concordance software can be used with the students' own texts to discover or highlight features of vocabulary and style.

Materials Computers, students' texts in machine-readable form, concordance software as needed.

Preparation

1 Build up a small corpus of student-generated text. This is best done over a period, in the course of normal classwork, by asking the class to do their written assignments on a computer, or to type fair copies

of handwritten work. Asking them to keep a 'public diary' or 'blog' (= web log) on computer is also a good way to collect texts.

2 Organize the texts in directories (folders), one for each student, and make sure that each classroom computer can access them and has the necessary concordance software.

Procedure

1 Ask the students to make frequency-ordered wordlists, first of the whole corpus, and then of only their own texts.

2 In groups of three to four they should compare the lists, and pick out words which occur much more, or much less, in their own texts than in all the texts taken together. (*Wordsmith Tools* has a 'keywords' function which will compare two frequency lists and list the anomalies automatically. See page 167.)

3 Encourage the students to look at these words in their original contexts, and to suggest possible changes to the language used.

Variation 1

If the texts were collected over a long period of time, say a year or more, organize them by date of composition, and ask the students to compare word-lists made from the earliest with wordlists from the latest, and to see if there are interesting differences in frequency. Are there words or phrases which they once used a lot, but which they now don't seem to be using at all?

Variation 2

In a mixed group, ask them to make two wordlists, one from the texts written by males, and the other from those written by females, and to compare the two.

Variation 3

Depending on the type and content of the texts, students can look at specific word types or semantic areas. In a collection of personal letters or emails, for example, it might be instructive to compare the relative frequency of *I/me/my* and *you/your*. A look at the use in descriptive texts of phrases such as *looks like*, *sounds like*, *feels like*, or at adjectives of colour, sound, and movement, may show clear differences between people who are primarily visual, auditory, or kinaesthetic.

Variation 4

If you have access to a large general corpus, such as the British National Corpus, you can ask the students to compare the relative frequencies of words and phrases in their own texts and in the larger corpus. If, for example, a student discovers that they have used the phrase *very nice* 10 times in their own 2000 words of text (i.e. 0.5%) and that *very nice* appears 700 times in the ca. 10-million-word spoken dialogue section of the BNC (i.e. 0.007%), they may decide to look round for a few alternative expressions.

5.7 Quarrying the Internet for words

Level Intermediate to advanced

Time 30–60 minutes in class, spread out over several sessions as necessary.

Aims To encourage students to learn how words and phrases are used by searching the Internet for example texts.

To give practice in using computers and software without losing sight of more immediate language learning needs.

Materials Computers, Internet access, concordance software as needed (see below).

Preparation

1 One or two lessons before you intend to do the activity, get the class to select a topic area that interests them and to brainstorm words and phrases which they expect to find in texts on the topic. Get them to reduce their list to five or six key items.

2 Open your browser and use a search engine such as Google or AltaVista to find on the web texts containing the words and phrases chosen. At this stage don't download any of the texts themselves, just the lists of web addresses (URLS). The first 10–20 addresses for each word or phrase, together with the textual context that is usually also given, will be ample. Save the lists if you need to interrupt the work.

3 Read through your lists of addresses: use the context information (the strings of text that contain the search words) to select 12–15 texts. Download them and save them to disk.

4 Use suitable software (for example, Wordlist in *WordSmith Tools*) to prepare wordlists for each text, and a combined word list for all the texts: these will show the words used in the texts together with the number of times they appear. Edit the word lists to exclude words that occur very frequently in the language, such as articles and pronouns. (The software will probably be able to do this automatically.) You may also like to re-edit and/or re-format the lists in a word processor.

5 Print out and make copies of the original texts and the word lists. You will need one copy or more of each text to put up on the walls or spread out on the tables, and each student will need one copy of *one* of the individual word lists and one copy of the combined word list. You should also have a few extra copies of each text for the students to read at home.

(Depending on the availability of computers and Internet access, and on the students' familiarity with the equipment and software, some or all of the above can be done by the students themselves. See the Comments below for ways of making the various processes involved more efficient.)

Procedure

1 Put up one copy of each text on the walls, or on flat surfaces where they can easily be seen and read. In larger classes, you may need to put up more than one copy of each text.

2 Give each student one copy of the word list for one of the texts. In smaller classes, each student should have a different word list.

3 Tell the students to look through their word list for a minute or two, and then to walk round and try to find the original text from which it was prepared. When they have done this, they should sit down and underline on their list all the words or phrases that they don't know, or which they would like more information about.

4 As more and more students finish steps 2 and 3, get them to form pairs or threes to discuss whether (a) they were surprised by the language or content of the text they found, and (b) the texts, as a whole, met the expectations they had when they first chose the search words or phrases that yielded them.

5 Ask the students to form groups of four to six and give each student a copy of the combined word list. Tell them to use the lists to help them produce a list of new words or phrases to search for, as in Preparation, step 1, above.

Variation 1

Instead of producing word lists, print out the words and phrases in contextualized format, as in the concordance extracts in activities 5.2, 5.3, and 5.4.

Variation 2

If you have computers available in the classroom, the students, in small groups, can look at a concordance listing directly on screen, speculate about the wider context (vocabulary, situation, etc.) of each extract, and then expand it to check their predictions. If the listing is based on a number of different texts, the filenames and line numbers can also be shown, making it very easy for the students to access a whole text that interests them and print it out for later reading.

Comments

To search the web, use your browser to access one of the many search engines available, type in the terms you wish to search for, wait to receive a page (or more often page upon page) of web addresses, and then click to access as many papers as you wish. However, you may have problems with the sheer quantity of information you have to wade through. How can you maximize your chances of quickly finding what you want, and how can you process it most efficiently once you've got it? Here are a few pointers:

1 If you are only interested in text, not pretty pictures, switch off your browser's 'fetch images automatically' option.

2 If you're fetching material for later study, and don't need to read it as it arrives at your computer, choose the 'Save to file' or 'Save to disk'

option; a lot of time can be wasted waiting for the text to appear on the screen.

3 If you're using an on-line search engine, check the options it offers: you may be able to restrict your search to a particular topic area ('Science', 'On-line Newspapers', and so on), to a particular language and/or country, or to a range of dates (for example, only files updated in the last year).

4 When searching for specific phrases, make sure you use the 'exact words' option. (This may be a button, a check-box, or require you to enclose the phrase in quotation marks.)

5 Not all search engines use the same search methods: what one fails to find may well be listed by another. Use different search engines, or try one of the 'metasearch' sites, which take your query, pass it on to several search engines, and combine the results before sending them back to you. One site of interest to us is http://webcorp.org.uk/wcadvanced.html, which can present search results either as a normal listing or as a concordance display.

6 Text is found on the Internet in different forms, and not all are easy to process in word-listing concordance software. Plain text files (.txt) present few problems, and most concordancers will deal with normal web pages, (.html, .htm). Word-processor files (.doc, .rtf and so on) may need to be loaded into the appropriate application first and saved as plain text, as will Portable Document Format (.pdf) and Powerpoint (.ppt) documents.

7 Many web pages contain the text you want, but a lot of other stuff as well: advertisements, navigation links and so on. When concordanced, such pages may give a false impression by showing repeated occurrences of *go to top*, *buy now*, and so on. If you have to work with these pages, you will have to use your browser's 'Save As' or 'Export' function to turn the file into plain text, and then, in a word processor, edit out all the unwanted material.

8 The book in this series by Scott Windeat, David Hardisty, and David Eastment entitled *The Internet* (2000) gives extensive guidance on the use of the Internet for language teachers.

6
Words and the senses

The sensory emphasis in coursebooks and classrooms is mainly on the visual channel of perception. Blackboards, wall-charts, book illustrations, and printed texts combine to produce a feast for the learners' eyes, but at the expense of those other channels which mediate experience, imagination, and memory. Nor is perception itself as simple as it might appear: at the neurological level, the sensory signals that we receive from, for example, the retina in our eye, make up less than a quarter of the information that our brain processes when presenting us with a 'visual image'—the rest is composed of memories, stored patterns, and learnt procedures. In a concrete sense, what we perceive and how we perceive it are largely the product of training and habit.

In the same way, our memories, whether of sensory impressions, procedures, or 'facts', will in turn be affected by the ways in which we have learnt to process reality. For many years, psychologists, neurologists, and other researchers in the human sciences have observed that we vary widely in our 'preferred channels' of perception, and that this has marked effects on how we learn, and on how we express ourselves. (For an early, but still influential account, see Bandler and Grinder 1975, which draws heavily on the work of the psychologist Gregory Bateson and the psychotherapist Milton Erickson.) Others, such as Howard Gardner at Harvard, have gone further, arguing for the existence of 'multiple intelligences' within us to explain differences of perception, behaviour, thought, and creativity. (See the Annotated Bibliography section at the end of this book for works by Gardner and others in this area.)

The implications of this for us as teachers are far-reaching, if not at present very clear. We can accept, however, that *how* material and information are presented to and worked on by our students will have a profound effect on their learning, and that in vocabulary learning, for example, the memorability of a word or collocation will, for any particular learner, depend on the settings in which it is encountered, the channels through which it is processed, and the type of intelligence (in Gardner's sense) into which it must be integrated. In this chapter, therefore, we offer activities that range across the sensory spectrum, and which allow the student to process and practise language in ways appropriate to their perceptual and cognitive preferences. These include not only visual and auditory activities, but also those that involve space and *movement* (kinaesthesia), as well as more abstract, logical exercises.

6.1 Words and our senses

Level **Lower-intermediate to advanced**

Time **25–40 minutes**

Aims **To make students aware of their own sensory preferences through the words they choose and the texts they respond most strongly to.**

Materials **A copy of the text for each student.**

Preparation

Make copies of the Sample sheet below, which consists of three descriptions of the same car accident, each written from a different sensory perspective.

Procedure

1 Read the three descriptions aloud to your class and ask them what differences they notice between them.

2 Read again and repeat your question.

Sample sheet

An accident

1 Swooping down to the right. Wet air rushing in through the windscreen. Back on to the motorway surface—grinding, shuddering along the central barrier. Over on two wheels. I am high, high. We are tipping? We sway for hours. Oomph, ooomph, down on four wheels and amazingly I am in control again. Veer over on to the hard shoulder and find I have stopped. A tingling of fine windscreen glass under my top skin.

2 I see the phone as it goes. Then there is a blank, like I'm not there, until I see cars coming the other way close, over the barrier. Everything looks tipped over—we are on two wheels. Now I can see everything clearly, the fog in my head has cleared and I steer us over to the hard shoulder. In the mirror I see cars pulling up behind. How must all that have looked to the people following us?

3 A sharp crack. Metal on metal. The muffled shattering of the windscreen powdering. Normal tyre roar and thud, thud, thud—we are back on the motorway. Screeching, scratching, scraping along the steel barrier. Bang bang, back on four wheels. And now like silence, stillness and wet air around me.

3 Give them copies of the texts to read for themselves.

4 Ask the students, working on their own, to weave the bits they like from each text into a new one, adding whatever they want themselves.

5 Tell them to circulate what they have written or to put it up on the walls, and to go round and read what the others have written.

Comments

The language that we use often reflects the way in which particular senses dominate our perceptions and thoughts: those of us who are primarily auditory, for example, may use a high proportion of *sound* words and metaphors. Similarly, we may respond better to language that matches our own sensory preferences. (Skilled interviewers and counsellors often use this to encourage people to talk.) In this activity, students are led to become aware of their preferences and to use them creatively.

6.2 Notion pictures

Level Beginner to intermediate

Time 20–30 minutes

Aims To review and recall vocabulary.

Materials Dictionaries.

Preparation

Choose a notion such as *joining*, *water things*, or *protection*. Take a large dictionary with you to class, especially if English is not your mother tongue.

Procedure

1 Exemplify the concept chosen by drawing: for *joining* this might be, say, a hinge, and a priest marrying two people.

2 Ask the students to draw as many things and people that *join* as they can. Let them work either on their own or in pairs.

3 Once the students have got a good number of drawings down on paper, and not before, ask them to label their drawings. They can use each other's knowledge, dictionaries, and you as an informant.

4 Ask the students to stand up and work in pairs, showing their drawings and teaching their words to other people. When they have finished with one partner, they should move on to another, rather than cluster in larger and larger groups. Stop the exercise when each person has worked with about five partners.

Example When we have done this exercise with *joining* as the concept word, students have produced drawings of the following:

crowd	river	dividing line
audience	apex	shelf
engagement ring	bread and butter	electric plug
cocktail	border	handcuffs
bridge	comma	

With *water things*, students have produced drawings of the following:

sprinkler	spirit level	tap
octopus	starfish	well
hosepipe	whale	river
estuary	irrigation	spring
gumboots	umbrella	bath tub
goggles	water meter	swimming pool

Comments

This activity is mainly visual. It is highly repeatable, especially if you, or your students, are willing to choose less obvious 'notions'.

6.3 Machines and scenes

Level **Elementary to advanced**

Time **30–40 minutes**

Aims **To provide visual and kinaesthetic ways of presenting and learning new vocabulary.**

Materials **Dictionary.**

Preparation

Make sure before you start that you are fully conversant with the words that may be called for by the students, so that you can supply them if asked. Have a dictionary handy in class.

Procedure

1 Find someone in the group who likes drawing and ask them to draw or diagram a given scene/machine/situation/process on the blackboard. Tell the artist to use the whole of the board.

2 Once the drawing has begun to take shape get someone in the group with clear handwriting to come out and start labelling what has been drawn. This should be done with the help of the group. As teacher, you should only supply a word when asked to: i.e. act as informant only.

3 Tell the students to copy the board drawing into their notebooks and to write the words in on the drawings: this makes more sense than writing lists of words.

4 The words now need to be used in a context beyond the picture. Three ways of doing this are suggested in the detailed Examples that follow.

Examples **Some word areas that lend themselves to this activity**

1 Tell the artist to draw a *bicycle*. Follow steps 1, 2, and 3 above in order to familiarize students with the necessary vocabulary. Then ask the students to look at the illustration below and to jot down all the differences they can see between the two bikes there. Ask the students to form pairs and compare the differences they have found—this will bring oral production of the words being learnt.

2 Tell the artist to draw the people working on a *building site*, with houses at different stages of completion. After doing steps 1, 2 and 3 above, ask the students a question such as *Can the plasterer work on the house before the bricklayer?* Then tell them to organize themselves into a line across the classroom representing the time sequence in which building workers work on a house. Each student (or pair of students in a large class) is to assume the role of one type of worker. You should take no part in this organization, except to keep them speaking in English.

3 Tell the artist to visualize the *dashboard and controls of a car*, as seen from the back seat, and to draw them. After the group has followed steps 1, 2 and 3 above, put two chairs out in front of them, side by side. Then invite one student to sit on one chair and play the part of a driving instructor, while you sit beside them and play the part of a slow pupil: show nervousness, and ask the instructor what each control is and what it is for. Then ask the whole class to act out the learner–instructor scene simultaneously in pairs.

As a follow-up activity, in a later class, ask the pairs to continue the scene into the first stages of a driving lesson: moving off and coming to a stop.

Comments

The exercises outlined here may be used in any situation involving the drawing and labelling of pictures, diagrams, plans, maps, etc.

6.4 Elephants

Level Elementary to advanced

Time 40–50 minutes

Aims To encourage peer-teaching both of subject-matter and of lexis.

Procedure

1 Ask each student to write down a list of 8 to 12 words that are central to their profession, or to a hobby or interest.

2 Ask the students to draw a picture of an animal, machine, etc. All the students should draw the same subject: choose something which is clear, easy to draw, and which has recognizably distinct parts (for example, *elephant*, *cat*, *bicycle*).

3 Ask each student to label the picture with the terms on their list from step 1: where to put the words on the picture is up to the student.

4 Form the students into small groups. They should in turn give mini-lectures on their chosen subjects, using their labelled picture as a visual aid.

Example One student who worked in photolithographic printing produced this elephant:

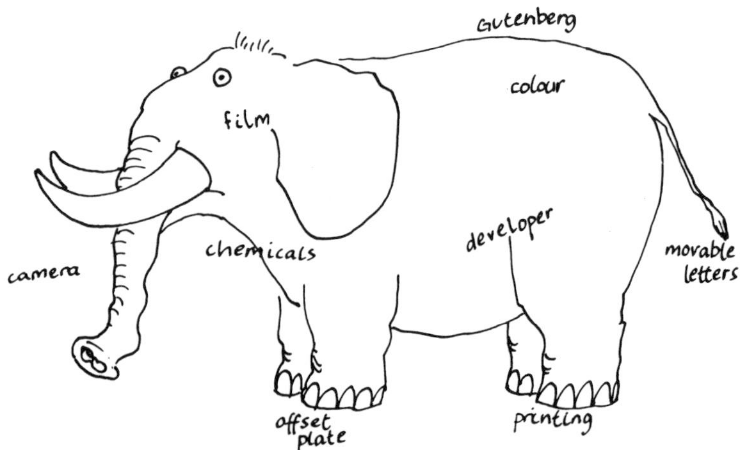

Comments

This exercise may at first sight seem strange. So it should, as it uses the principle of 'making strange' what is familiar. Having to place the words from your list on the elephant forces you to look at them from a new angle. Looking at and listening to another person doing the same makes what they have to say, and the words they use to say it, memorable.

6.5 Exploring vocabulary kinaesthetically

Level Beginner to advanced

Time 15–30 minutes, depending on class size.

Aims To learn vocabulary through movement.

Procedure

With an upper-intermediate class you might choose to teach the names of trees:

1. Bring the students together in a big standing circle. (This may have to be in among the desks, if they are fixed.)
2. Ask one of the students to bring to mind a tree. This must be a particular kind of tree, and the student should then mime the way *that* tree would be: the student mimes silently and everybody round the circle mirrors the mime.
3. The student next round the circle mimes a tree they have in mind. Everybody mirrors them. And so on round the circle, or if your class is large, round part of the circle.
4. Go back to the first student, who mimes their tree again and says the word for it in the target language if they can, otherwise in their mother tongue. (You or the dictionary give the target-language version.)
5. Proceed round the group like this. Have a student at the board writing down the words in both languages, until all the tree names are up on the board.
6. The students return to their seats and copy the words into their notebooks, adding the mother-tongue word and, if they wish, a quick drawing.

Variations

At beginner level you can have students deal with a word field such as *animals*; lower-intermediate students can deal with *weather words* (for example, *mist, breeze, gale, frost*—how would you mime being '*frost*'?). Advanced-level students can work with abstract words in a given area, for example, *truth, deception, sincerity, shallowness, distrust*. (This produces much more revealing mimes than *trees*.)

Comments

This technique harnesses the kinaesthetic and the visual abilities of the learners. It gets the students out of their seats and allows them to move, something that is *essential* for a minority of them. In multiple intelligence terms (see the beginning of this chapter), it simultaneously activates the kinaesthetic/spatial and linguistic intelligences.

6.6 Coins speak

Level Elementary to advanced

Time 15–25 minutes

Aims To explore the spatial and hierarchical associations of words, as an aid to understanding and memory.

Materials A collection of identical small objects, such as counters, coins, buttons. You will need around ten per student. You will also need one sheet of white paper for each pair of students.

Preparation

1 Prepare an introductory list of words with a strong spatial or hierarchical sense for the students to practise on, for example,

airport beach village field forest school garage
or
class crowd regiment queue party club junta

2 Prepare a list or lists of words you would like the students to work on: these should be words with a strong emotional or controversial content, for example,

guilt independence innocence revenge contradiction ingratitude age stability sadness hostility death

Procedure

1 Ask the students to form groups of three to four.

2 Give them your list of spatial/hierarchical words. Make sure they check with dictionaries or by asking that they understand them all.

3 Give each group a pile of 15–25 counters or coins, and a sheet of plain white paper to arrange them on.

4 Ask one student in each group to select a word from the list and then, without saying which word they have chosen, to represent the word by means of an arrangement of counters or coins on the paper.

5 When the first student has done this, the others in the group should try to guess which word was selected.

6 After each member of the group has selected and represented one word from the introductory list, introduce the second set of emotional words and ask them to continue working on them. Stop the exercise after two or three more rounds.

Examples

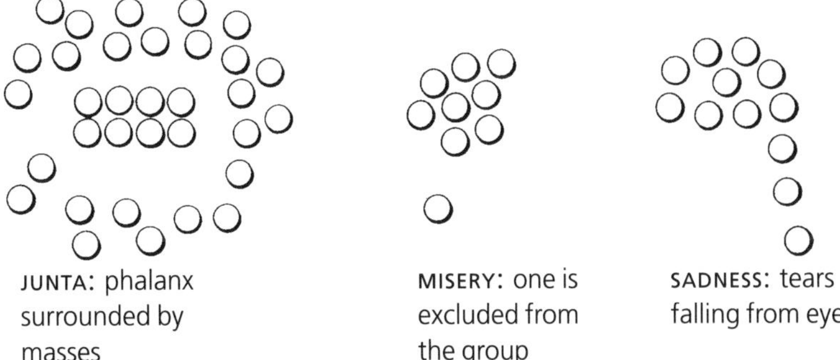

JUNTA: phalanx surrounded by masses

MISERY: one is excluded from the group

SADNESS: tears falling from eye

Variation 1

After the introductory stage, ask the students to write their own lists of words that are important or exciting or disturbing for them, and to work in pairs on these. This exercise can be repeated many times during a course with whatever vocabulary happens to be under consideration: even abstract words can have powerful spatial associations for many people.

Variation 2

The exercise can equally well be used as a pre-reading exercise. It then has the double value of exploring vocabulary from the text, and getting the readers to think through their own ideas/prejudices before reading.

6.7 Picture gallery

Level Elementary to advanced

Time 35–50 minutes

Aims 1 To get students to use known (or half-known) vocabulary in new situations, and to learn vocabulary from each other.

2 To get students to write texts that other students will want to read.

Materials A collection of magazine pictures (see Preparation).

Preparation

Collect magazine pictures with a strong direct impact, visually uncluttered—portions are often more useful than whole pictures. Select enough pictures for each member of the class to have two. Make a varied selection: don't choose only pictures that *you* like. Take Blu-Tack, or some other means of fixing the pictures to the walls.

Procedure

1 Split the class into two equal groups, one at each end of the room. Spread out half the pictures for one group and half for the other group.

2 Ask each student to choose a picture, but not to show it to anyone in the other group. Remove any unchosen pictures.
3 Ask the students to write clearly on a piece of paper twelve words suggested by the picture they have chosen. Ban adjectives.
4 When everyone has finished, take away each student's picture and ask everyone to lay out their sheets of words at their end of the room.
5 Ask the students to change ends and choose one list from those written by the other group.
6 Ask them to read their word lists and then to write a short paragraph describing the picture they imagine behind the words.
7 When they have done this, put up the pictures around the walls, and ask the students to look round for the picture that best corresponds to the list they have worked from and to put up their paragraph and the word list next to it.
8 Invite the students to go round and look at the pictures and read the compositions.

Example A student in one group chose a picture of a detail cut from a magazine advertisement: the skin on a woman's stomach glistening with beads of moisture; her well-manicured hand is on her stomach, above the navel; a fine gold chain encircles her stomach. The student wrote this list of words suggested by the picture:

> finger smooth skin bath red nails woman chain
> stomach water play hair navel

A student from the other group wrote this paragraph, suggested by the word list:

> A woman was lying in the bath. She has smooth skin. You can see her stomach and she was playing with a chain and you can also see her nails which reflect your eyes.

Comments

This is a mainly visual activity. See 3.1, 'Invisible writing'.

6.8 Listening in colour

Level **Elementary to advanced**
Time **15 minutes**
Aims **To learn vocabulary through specific visual associations.**
Materials **A poster or other large, colourful picture.**

Preparation

Choose a brightly coloured painting or poster in which there is plenty of action. It should not be too complicated. Prepare to describe the picture without mentioning any colour.

Procedure

1 Put the picture or poster up somewhere the class can't see it. Tell them that the picture is highly coloured, but that they will have to imagine the colours for themselves. Then describe the picture in full spatial detail, but without mentioning any colour.

2 Ask people to tell the class which colours they saw. They should be as specific as possible.

3 Show the class the picture. Points such as these may come up in general discussion:

- how the painter felt when s/he painted it
- what kind of painter s/he was/is
- what kind of room it would suit
- would you like it in your house?

Variation

Instead of using a picture, you can tell a story, taking care not to use any reference to colour in your descriptions. Then ask the students to re-tell the story in colour, for example, *The dark-eyed girl put on her blue coat ....*

Comments

Our visual perception is very complicated, and even those of us who are 'highly visual' may differ markedly in how we visualize. Colour, for example, may be vitally important for some; for others line, shape, or proportion may dominate.

Acknowledgements

This idea appeared in an article by Malgorzata Szwaj in *Modern English Teacher* in 1984.

6.9 Get as much wrong as you can

Level Upper-intermediate to advanced

Time 10–20 minutes

Aims To meet head-on the challenge of linking the meanings of words with their visual and auditory representations.

Materials A copy of the text for each student.

Preparation

Make copies of the short passage included at step 4 below.

Procedure

1 Explain to the class that you are going to give them a dictation and that every time they *hear/here* a homophone they are to *write/right* down the written version that is wrong for the context.

To make the idea of homophone clear, write up a few on the board:

I'll	aisle	isle	
sort	sought*		
freeze	frees	frieze	
or	ore	oar	awe*
sees	Cs	seas	seize

(Words marked * are homophonic only in those dialects where end-of-syllable 'r' is not sounded, such as British RP.)

Offer a small prize for the student with the most 'mistakes'.

2 Give this dictation and do it slowly:

Homophones are an odd phenomenon. Take the word *site*, which can mean a location, or the ability to see, or the act of quoting. We tend to exclude the meaning that is not contextually right. If you did not do this, you would go barmy. So, to be able to shut out unwanted meanings is part of being sane.

3 Group the students in fours to share homophones they were aware of.

4 Give out the homophonic text below for them to compare their own with.

> Homophones are a nod phenomenon. Take the whirred *site/sight/cite*, witch can mean a plaice, ore the ability to sea, oar the act of quoting. Wee tend to exclude the meaning that is knot contextually write. If yew did knot do this ewe wood go balmy*. Sow/Sew, to bee able to shut out the unwanted meanings is part of being seine. (a *seine* net, or the River *Seine*)

Variation

For homework, ask three or four of your more linguistically-interested students to go to homophone sites on the web and then to produce short texts like the one above, which include plenty of homophonic words.

If four students have done this homework, divide the class up into four groups, so that each group takes a homophonic dictation from one of the students. A good site for this homework is http://www.peak.org/-jeremy/dictionary/homophones.html

Comments

1 For many classroom learners, having to learn the spoken and written forms of a language at the same time makes things doubly difficult, not least because this involves the simultaneous exercise of auditory and visual skills, in either or both of which they may be deficient.

2 The principle of treating errors as interesting rather than wicked is fundamental to non-behaviourist teaching.

Acknowledgements

We learnt the idea of *une dictée sans fautes* oar *une dictée cents fautes* (*dictation without mistakes*, or *one-hundred-mistake dictation*) from the *fiches pédagogiques* in *Le Français dans le Monde*, February 2000.

6.10 OHP lists

Level Beginner to advanced

Time 10–15 minutes

Aims To break up the order and visual monotony of lists as an aid to memory.

Materials Overhead projector and transparencies.

Preparation

1 Make a list of 10–15 target-language words or phrases that you want your students to learn or revise, or ask them to give you short lists of words or phrases they are having difficulty in remembering, and make your selection from them.

2 Write the words on an overhead transparency in black, in two neat columns.

3 Write the words again on another transparency, but this time scatter them all over the sheet. Use different coloured inks, different sizes and styles of lettering. Write some of the words at an angle, or backwards, or around the circumference of a circle.

4 Prepare three more transparencies as in step 3, using the same words or phrases but writing them differently on each sheet. Be adventurous.

Procedure

1 Put up the first transparency (the neat one in black lettering). Allow the students to look at it for 10–15 seconds, then switch it off.

2 Ask the students to jot down any words they remember and for each to add a brief explanation or mother-tongue equivalent, from memory or by guesswork.

3 Give the class five minutes to compare and discuss the words they have jotted down. If the words are new to them, you may want to join in at this stage to give explanations and examples.

4 Tell the students to put away their written notes and to concentrate on the screen. Flash up all five transparencies in turn, each for 10–15 seconds.

5 Ask the students, in groups of three to five, to recall each word or phrase and to discuss which visual representation of it was the most memorable.

Variation

Instead of an overhead projector, you could use a computer + video projector and present your lists using one of the many software 'presentation packages' such as PowerPoint or Shockwave. (In these cases, you could even add a soundtrack!)

Follow-up

This is a highly repeatable activity. Once the students have understood the process, you can get them to prepare the OP transparencies for their own use, or to use with students in other classes.

Comments

For some people, words presented in neat lists can be memorable. For many, however, the very neatness makes it difficult to bring back a picture of what they have read: our visual memory often depends on the unusual, the unexpected. Scattering words on a page or blackboard or overhead projector transparency can be very helpful in giving students signposts to their memories.

This technique is particularly useful in preparing students for exams.

6.11 Words round the circle

Level **Beginner to intermediate**

Time **10–15 minutes**

Aims **To practise saying words using the full vocal range.**

Preparation

Choose 10–12 useful collocations from your coursebook or elsewhere.

Procedure

1 Get the students standing in a large circle right round the classroom.

2 Number them off *1 2 3 4 5 6 7 8 ... 1 2 3 4 etc.*

3 On the board write:

All 1s to whisper.
All 2s to call out loudly.
All 3s to speak slowly.
All 4s to speak fast.
All 5s to mouth without sound.
All 6s to sing.
All 7s to speak in a shrill voice.
All 8s to speak in their mother tongue.

4 Explain that you are going to take one of the collocations chosen in your hands and then both say it and *hand it to* the person on your right. This person holds out their hands and takes the collocation, then turns to the person on the right and gives it into their hands and says it in the way suggested above, whispering, singing, etc.... Thus

the collocation goes right round the circle as an 'object' and as an ever-changing sequence of sounds.

5 Do the exercise round the circle. If any student makes a mess of pronouncing the phrase, walk over to the person 'downstream' of them (to their right), and give the phrase back to the person on the mistake-maker's left, who then again gives it to the mistake-maker. This allows the person with the problem to hear the sounds twice again before re-pronouncing them.

6 Any student unsure of the pronunciation of the phrase can cross the circle and give you the phrase. You give it back and say it to the person, who then goes back to their place in the circle to continue the chain.

Variation

This can also be done as a follow-up.

1 Get the students to work in circles of 6–12.

2 Ask them to work as in the activity above, but to choose for themselves the best or most interesting way (shouting, whispering, etc.) of saying each item.

Comments

This activity is both highly auditory and kinaesthetic, and has proved very useful in teaching adult immigrants without literacy skills.

6.12 Filling a landscape

Level **Beginner to advanced**

Time **3 minutes in the first class, 10 minutes in the second.**

Aims **To encourage students to discover vocabulary for themselves and to teach it to others.**

Materials **Photocopies of a picture for each student.**

Preparation

Choose a picture with strong contrasts, such as a Breughel snowscape, that will photocopy clearly. Make a copy for each student.

In the first class

Give out the copies. Ask the students for homework to write on the picture any words it suggests. These may be labellings of features that are there or they may be words suggested by the feel and mood of the picture. Encourage students to use dictionaries to find the words they want. Tell them they must be willing to teach any new words they have used.

In the second class

Put the students in fours to compare the words they have found: a lot of peer teaching will follow.

Variation 1

The same exercise can of course be done with the students' own pictures, but this often has the effect of lessening the peer teaching aspect: one may be more interested in the different way in which someone else has seen the *same* picture, than in their reactions to a completely different picture.

Variation 2

Instead of asking the students to focus on what they can see in the picture, get them to speculate on what they cannot see: things which may be hidden behind other things, things which are outside the frame of the picture, things or people which were there before the picture was painted, or which the artist decided to leave out.

Comments

Peer teaching is an excellent way of learning. The activity is primarily visual.

6.13 Fishy adjectives

Level Intermediate to advanced

Time 30–40 minutes

Aims To use, in a creative, memorable way, adjectives that describe people.

Materials Copies of either Worksheet 1 or Worksheet 2 for each student. (See pages 97–8.)

Procedure

Ask the students to follow the instructions of whichever worksheet you give them.

Acknowledgements

We learnt this exercise from Lou Spaventa.

Worksheet 1

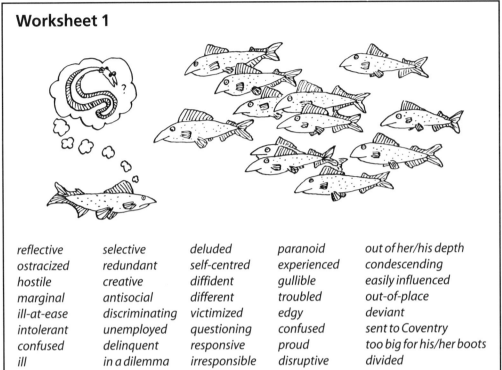

reflective	*selective*	*deluded*	*paranoid*	*out of her/his depth*
ostracized	*redundant*	*self-centred*	*experienced*	*condescending*
hostile	*creative*	*diffident*	*gullible*	*easily influenced*
marginal	*antisocial*	*different*	*troubled*	*out-of-place*
ill-at-ease	*discriminating*	*victimized*	*edgy*	*deviant*
intolerant	*unemployed*	*questioning*	*confused*	*sent to Coventry*
confused	*delinquent*	*responsive*	*proud*	*too big for his/her boots*
ill	*in a dilemma*	*irresponsible*	*disruptive*	*divided*
subversive				

1 If you were one of the fish in the shoal, which one would you be? Put a tick by it.

2 What three things might you say to the rest of the fish in the shoal about the fish in the bottom left-hand corner? Write your answers:

____

____

____

3 Pick 10–15 adjectives and phrases from the list above, or from your head, to describe the fish that is out of the shoal. Look up any words from the list you don't know, or ask your neighbour.

4 Work in pairs with several different people in the group to find how and why they chose their adjectives.

5 Talk to your partner about anyone you know who is like the fish outside the shoal, and about how they show it.

Worksheet 2

1 Give all these fish nicknames and write them down.
2 Which fish would you most like to be?
3 Which fish would you most hate to be?
4 Jot down ten adjectives to describe the fish you most like and ten to describe the one you like least.
5 Compare your answers with your neighbours'.

6.14 Objects round the circle

Level **Beginner to upper-intermediate**

Time **10–12 minutes**

Aims **To encourage students to express meaning in any way that suits them (visually, through movement, etc.), and then to ask for and learn the specific vocabulary they need.**

Preparation

None, since the purpose is to work on the students' own areas of interest. (You may, however, find yourself doing quite a lot of follow-up work, especially if their interests differ widely from yours!)

Procedure

1 Get the students into a big standing circle. Ask them to think of a piece of sporting equipment and imagine they are holding it in their hands. (It could be a baseball bat, a football, a golf tee, a fishing rod, etc.) The student with the object in their hands should feel its weight, texture, and temperature.

2 Ask one student, A, to show their object and then to hand it, without saying anything, to B, their right-hand neighbour.

3 Student B receives the object, guesses what it is, and passes it silently on to C, who is one away to their right. Alternatively B may change the object received into some other sporting object before passing it on to C.

4 Continue on round the circle.

5 Have a secretary at the board and ask A what they gave to B. If A doesn't know the word in English, then they say it in their mother tongue and you or a dictionary translates it. The secretary puts either or both words up on the board.

6 B now says what they received and then what they passed on. C does the same.

7 And so on round the circle. To get the students more into the reality of the objects, sometimes stop the student who is speaking and ask them about the weight, size, and colour of what they were receiving and passing.

8 The students sit down and an artistic one comes to the board and draws quick sketches of each item. The others copy down the words and the sketches.

6.15 Picturing words and phrases

Level **Elementary to advanced**

Time **20–30 minutes**

Aims **To use detailed, creative visualization to associate with the English words the students are learning.**

Preparation

Choose eight to twelve words and phrases you want the students to go into more deeply.

Procedure

1 (Optional.) Ask the students to shut their eyes and notice their breathing. Ask them to imagine that they are breathing stress and anxiety out and energy in. (The first time you do this with teenage classes be ready for giggling and noise.)

2 Say the words and phrases you have chosen aloud, leaving a 10- to 20-second pause after each. Ask the students to make pictures in their mind's eye as they hear each word or phrase.

3 Bring the students back from their reverie, say again one of the words and phrases, and ask a student of your choice all or some of the following questions. Tell the other students to note down the questions you ask:

How big was the picture you got?
How close was the picture to you?
Were you inside the picture, or outside looking in?
Was it in black and white or in colour?

Was it moving or still?
What, exactly, did you see?

During this stage, students who did not understand some of the dictated words will have an opportunity to find out or ask about them.

4 Choose another word from the list and put the same questions to another student. Repeat with a third person.

5 Pair the students and ask them to explore the pictures they got for the words, using the questions you asked in step 3.

7
Word sets

There are many practical reasons for organizing words (or, more often, what the words refer to) into categories, or sets, or 'word fields'. A supermarket without shelf labels would be a nightmare to navigate, and it is a great help to the curriculum designer and the coursebook writer to split up the vocabulary the student is expected to learn into 'topic areas'. Linguists also like to work with word sets, not only grammatical categories, but meaning groups (synonyms or near-synonyms), ideas of 'concrete' and 'abstract', 'animate' and 'inanimate', words of a particular origin or register, and so on.

In relation to learning, however, things work out rather less efficiently. We do not always agree about the categories we set up: we divide up the world, and the words we use to describe it, in quite different ways, according to our culture, our upbringing, our mother tongue, and our personal experiences and thought processes. Moreover, the categories that we use to describe things, or to find things in supermarkets and reference books, do not necessarily correspond to the needs of learning and memory: very often we remember things because they are unusual, and do not fit into a category, and we forget things or muddle them up precisely because they *do* fit into a category, and lose distinctive, memorable features thereby.

In this chapter, therefore, we have collected a dozen or so exercises which deal with word sets in challenging, unorthodox ways, in which the students are encouraged to question, compare, and build vocabulary sets for themselves. Some offer new ways of handling ready-made sets (for example, 7.1, 'Intelligence test', and 7.8, 'Prototypes'); others suggest personal, even surreal ways of grouping words (for example, 7.6, 'Diagonal opposites', 7.10, 'Mapping one's mood'), while 7.4, 'Collecting collocations', and 7.9, 'Words from the homestay family', suggest ways in which the students can learn from their own observations of language.

7.1 Intelligence test

Level **Beginner to intermediate**

Time **10 minutes**

Aims **To explore the idea of a 'word set' and the many different ways in which one can categorize vocabulary.**

Procedure

1 Put up the following items on the blackboard, explaining or illustrating where necessary.

pliers hammer nail saw

2 Ask the students to write down the odd man out and give their reason(s). When they have done this, ask for their suggestions. Then tell them that the 'right answer' is *pliers*, because it is the only one with two legs. If there are many 'incorrect' answers, a discussion on the validity of such tests might well ensue.

3 Now ask the group to make as many sets as possible using two or more of the items in the list *pliers*, *hammer*, *nail*, *saw*.

Examples *all metal*: nail hammer pliers
aggressive/active: pliers saw hammer
nail set: nail hammer pliers
could be verbs/are grammatically singular: hammer nail saw
tools: hammer pliers saw
one syllable: nail saw
-er ending (agent form): hammer pliers
Germanic origin: hammer saw nail

7.2 Unusual word families

Level **Elementary to advanced**

Time **10 minutes for most of the suggestions below.**

Aims **To encourage students to group words in unusual, memorable categories.**

Procedure

Use only one of these student-directed suggestions in any given lesson:

a Work in pairs and list things found in an office but *not* in a home.
b Besides the sex differences, how can you tell your father and mother apart? List the most salient physical and emotional differences. Do the work alone, then explain your list to a partner you trust.
c Work with a partner. List the differences between your car/bicycle and theirs.

d Here is a list of common verbs:

clean listen heat taste squeeze push tap open

Work in pairs and think of three typical doers of each action and one atypical one. For example:

clean: typical: laundryman/painter/dentist
atypical: tramp

Compare your lists with those of other pairs.

e Work together in fours. One person should think of a place, building, or room, and tell the others three things that would be found there. The others should then try and guess the place. For example:

STUDENT A *(thinking of a library)*: shelf sunblind catalogue
STUDENT B: A lawyer's office?
STUDENT C: A supermarket?
STUDENT D: Here's an extra word: *book* ...

7.3 Chains

Level Elementary to advanced

Time 20 minutes

Aims To encourage students to group words in imaginative and memorable ways.

Materials One word card for each student.

Preparation

Prepare a card for each student. On each card write the name of one man-made object (for example, *sweater*, *book*, *sewing-machine*).

Procedure

1. Divide the class into small circles (four to five members). Give each student a word card.
2. Ask the students to look at the word on their card and to write either the name of something that went into the making of the object in front of the word, or the name of something that the object might become after the word. For example, if the word was *sweater*, one might write *sheep* before it or *paper* after it.
3. Each student should then pass the card to their left-hand neighbour, who should again write a word before or after the two words now on the card, for example, *grass sheep sweater*.

Variation

Instead of arranging the chain in a linear fashion, a tree could be built, with each student in turn adding a link, for example,:

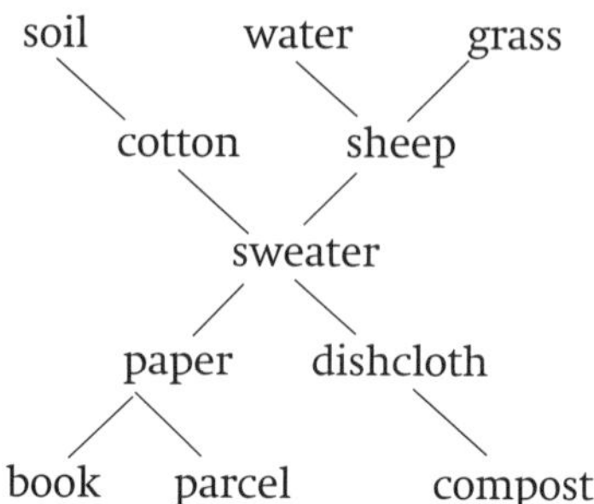

7.4 Collecting collocations

Level **Intermediate to advanced**

Time **5 minutes in the first lesson; 30–40 minutes in the second.**

Aims **To expand students' understanding and acquisition of above-the-word vocabulary.**

Materials **Enough English-language newspapers and magazines (old ones will do) to be able to give at least half of one to each student. A page or two is not enough for this activity.**

Procedure

Lesson 1

Give each student a newspaper or half a newspaper. Ask them for homework to pick out adjective-noun combinations where at least one item is new to them, or else their juxtaposition is. Ask them to find six such combinations each and to prepare to teach their meanings to the rest of the class. This may well mean bringing in the context in which they found them. Stress that they must be able to teach their collocations clearly and briefly.

Lesson 2

1 Divide the board into eight columns and invite a student to put one of their combinations in the first two columns and to teach it to the class. Then ask the group to produce other nouns that combine well with that adjective. Suppose a student volunteers a combination such as *FORTHCOMING EVENT*—the columns might well look like this:

adjective	noun	noun	noun	noun	noun	noun	noun
forthcoming	*event*	*sale*	*marriage*	*issue*	*publication*	*strike?*	*debut*

If a person in the group comes up with a dubious companion for *FORTHCOMING* like *strike*, let the students thrash it out as far as possible among themselves—do not make a ruling for them, *ex cathedra*.

2 Invite different students to volunteer and teach one of their six combinations, until the board is full.

Variation

1 Many other combinations can be worked on, using the same method. Here are some of them:

noun–noun:	*tax burden*
	dancing master
adverb–adjective:	*unfortunately misleading*
	vastly complicated
adverb–verb:	*greatly to be regretted*
	inevitably flowed from
verb–adverb:	*vary greatly*
	replied huffily

2 Put a list of twenty nouns and ten verbs on the board. The students copy down the lists and supply each noun with a typical adjective and each verb with a typical adverb, for example:

an eccentric *millionaire*
to kiss lovingly

Comments

If you have access to a corpus of English and a concordance program (see Chapter 5), you can use this to check out the frequency of word combinations. Alternatively, you can use a good Internet search engine (such as Google) for the occurrence of particular combinations in web pages: make sure that you specify 'exact words' when you enter the search phrase (for example, by enclosing the phrase between double quotation marks).

Acknowledgements

We learnt this technique from Mike Lavery.

7.5 How strong is the collocation?

Level Upper-intermediate to advanced

Time 20–30 minutes

Aims To expand students' understanding and acquisition of above-the-word vocabulary.

Preparation

Choose a number of words closely related in meaning and/or context, and make a grid like the example below.

Procedure

1 Put this collocational grid on the board and ask the students to copy it out into their books. Write it up without the +/—/? marks you have on the next page: they give you, the teacher, the key.

	unblemished	spotless	flawless	immaculate	impeccable
performance	—	—	+	+	+
argument	—	—	+	—	?
complexion	?	?	+	—	—
behaviour	—	—	—	—	+
kitchen	—	+	—	+	—
record	+	+	—	?	+
reputation	+	+	—	+	?
taste	—	—	?	?	+
order	—	—	?	+	+
credentials	—	—	—	—	+

2 Ask the students to look the adjectives above up in their dictionaries. Ask them to put some definitions/translations up on the board.

3 Pair the students and explain that:

 spotless collocates strongly with *kitchen* and with *record* (+)
 spotless collocates weakly with *complexion* (?)
 spotless does not collocate with *order* (—)

4 Pair the students and ask them to decide which of the adjectives along the top collocate strongly, weakly, or not at all with the nouns down the left hand side. They mark (+) for a strong collocation, (?) for a weak one, and (—) for zero collocation.

5 Put the pairs together in sixes to compare their findings.

6 Give your book to a student to put the key up on the board.

Variation 1

This activity can be supplemented with web searches and concordance look-ups, though in the latter case there may not be sufficient data to come to firm conclusions, as many of the items will be of comparatively low frequency in the corpus used.

Variation 2

Advanced students may benefit from deliberately experimenting with atypical collocations, as a way of generating more imaginative, and less cliché-ridden, text.

Acknowledgements

We owe this exercise to a brilliant book by Mona Baker. *In Other Words, a Coursebook on Translation*. Routledge, 1992, from an original idea in Rudska, *et al. The Words You Need*. Macmillan, 1982.

7.6 Diagonal opposites

Level Beginner to intermediate

Time 10 minutes

Aims To get students to look closely at the semantic and situational associations of a word, and thus fix new vocabulary very firmly.

Materials A soft ball.

Procedure

1 Put up on the blackboard three or four words with clear opposites, for example, *cold, sad, rise*. Ask the class to suggest opposites for them.

2 Add two or three words that do not have clear opposites, for example, *ball, typewriter, Wednesday*. Suggest that by using the personal associations of words one can give these 'opposites' too. For example, *ball/mouse* are opposites because both are cats' playthings—the one dead, the other alive.

3 Ask the class to form circles of six to ten people. Give each group a ball. The first player takes the ball, shouts out a word, then throws the ball to another member of the circle. The second player shouts out an 'opposite', then a new word, and throws the ball to a third player. Let the game continue until twenty words have been dealt with.

Acknowledgements

We learnt the ball-game version from an internal publication brought out by Volkshochschule teachers of French in Lower Saxony, Germany.

7.7 The egg exercise

Level Beginner to advanced

Time 20 minutes

Aims To explore the various meanings and associations of a word or phrase.

Procedure

1 Ask the students, working on their own, to complete the following sentence stems as variedly and in as many ways as they can: at least seven completions for each sentence:

An egg ______________________________

Eggs ______________________________

It's hard to ______________ eggs ______________

2 Have a student come to the board and act as group secretary. The students shout out all the nouns and verbs they have used in their completions. Fill the board with the students' lexis.

3 In fours the students read out their sentences to each other.

Follow-up

This activity can be used over and over again to explore or fix the meanings of new vocabulary. Simply replace *egg* by the new item, for example, *A grandmother* [is a child's best friend], *It's hard to* [oppose] *grandmothers*.

7.8 Prototypes

Level **Beginner to advanced**

(The example set below is for lower-intermediate.)

Time **20–30 minutes**

Aims **To get students to consider how word sets are built up, by asking such questions as 'How strongly does this word belong to its set?', and in so doing to consider how effective for them such categorizations are in organizing and remembering vocabulary.**

Preparation

Find or construct sets of words, as in the examples below.

Procedure

1 Ask each student to take a clean sheet of paper and to write *weather* right in the middle of it.

2 They then draw five or six concentric circles round the word, the outer one reaching the edge of the paper.

3 Tell the students you are going to dictate a number of words to them to do with *weather*. If the students regard these as very centrally *weather* words, they put them in the inner circles. If they regard them as peripheral weather words, they put them in the outer areas. Here is a list:

to rain	blustery showers	drought	barometer
to snow	bright intervals	storm	outlook
temperature	dawn	overcast	lull
dry	unsettled	bright	fog
to pour	sunshine	to blow	breeze
to clear up	low pressure	forecast	force-eight wind
earthquake	rain or shine	damp	scorching
flood	downpour	sand storm	hurricane
the sun	cloud	sky	moon

4 Check that all the words you dictated are known to at least some of the students.

5 Group the students in fours to share their placing of the vocabulary, in terms of how centrally 'weatherish' they feel the words are. The words at the very centre of their circles could be called 'prototypes'—the members most typical of their set.

Variations

1 You can do this 'prototype' exercise with any word set, for example:

Which males in the following list are most male?

bull ogre dog stag tomcat drake boar ram
billygoat cock man elephant stallion gander cockerel

Which are the most 'foody' of these foods? Which the least?

tapioca cheese rice potatoes lamb snake burger
cucumber trout chips artichoke banana flour

2 A roleplay: choose, or get the students to choose, a set of words such as *birds*, *houses*, *carnivores*. Each student should then choose a different member of the set and be prepared to speak on its behalf. For example, if *birds* were the set chosen, one student might choose *falcon*, another *pigeon*, a third *chicken*, and so on. The students then each give a one-minute talk about the set member they have chosen, in which they try to convince the rest that their choice is prototypical of the whole set. This is done most effectively when the students give their talks *in role*, i.e. they might begin 'I am a falcon. I am light, powerful, and very fast' rather than 'I've chosen the falcon. A falcon is light, powerful, and very fast.'

3 (Advanced) The degree of 'prototypicality' of words may also become apparent in a text. Ask your students, in groups of three, to read the following extract and underline five to eight nouns in it. Working together, they should then write each underlined word down and next to it the name of a set to which the word might belong, followed by three or four other words that might belong to the same set. They should then read and re-read the text aloud, replacing each of the underlined words in turn by a different member of the set, and discuss the effect of their substitutions.

Sample text 1

Frightened people never learn, I have read. If that is so, they certainly have no right to teach. I'm not a frightened man—or no more frightened than any other man who has looked at death and knows it is for him. All the same, experience and a little pain had made me a mite too wary of the truth, even towards myself. George Smiley put that right. George was more than a mentor to me, more than a friend. Though not always present, he presided over my life. There were times when I thought of him as some kind of father to replace the one I never knew. George's visit to Sarratt gave back the dangerous edge to my memory. And now that I have the leisure to remember, that's what I mean to do for you, so that you can share my voyage and ask yourself the same questions.

(John le Carré. *The Secret Pilgrim*. Hodder & Stoughton, 1991)

Try out different kinds of text: newspaper article, coursebook passage, business letter, etc. The students may also like to work with texts they have written themselves.

Using the technique with poems can also bring unexpected insights into the perceptions of both poet and reader:

Sample text 2 **Home is so Sad**

Home is so sad. It stays as it was left,
Shaped to the comfort of the last to go
As if to win them back. Instead, bereft
Of anyone to please, it withers so,
Having no heart to put aside the theft

And turn again to what it started as,
A joyous shot at how things ought to be,
Long fallen wide. You can see how it was:
Look at the pictures and the cutlery,
The music in the piano stool. That vase.

(Philip Larkin. *The Whitsun Weddings*. Faber & Faber, 1964)

Comments

In logic and mathematics, sets are defined precisely in terms of the common properties of their members. In the real world, the sets or categories we construct are far less precise. Even conventional word sets, such as *furniture* and *fruit*, include and exclude members according to criteria that are far from clear. A *pear* is obviously a fruit, along with an *apple*, an *orange*, and a *banana*. For the botanist, so is a *tomato*, though few tomato-eaters would agree. For them, it is a *vegetable*, along with *peas*, *potatoes*, and *cabbage*. A *cupboard* is definitely a piece of furniture, but a *built-in cupboard* is definitely not. Because it is immovable? Perhaps, but the seats one finds in airports and concert-halls, screwed to the floor and often to each other, are just as much *furniture* as the *armchairs* and *dining-chairs* in our homes.

Acknowledgements

We learnt the idea of 'prototype' from Aitchison (1994).

7.9 Words from the homestay family

Level **Beginner to advanced**

(The vocabulary in the example given is intermediate.)

Time **2–3 minutes in the first lesson; 20–30 minutes in the second lesson.**

Aims **To provide a simple research tool for students studying in an English-speaking environment and living in host families.**

Lesson 1

For homework, ask the students to get their hosts to take them into the kitchen and teach them the names of all the utensils and the various verbs connected with cooking. Each student should come to the next lesson with a substantial list.

Lesson 2

1 Get the students to fill the board with their cooking words.

2 Get students to explain any of the words the others don't know.

3 Show the students how many of the kitchen verbs have strong metaphorical meanings:

Her anger boiled over.	He was simmering with rage.
Cool as a cucumber.	To stew in your own juice.

Variation 1

There are many other areas in which the students can quarry vocabulary from the host family, for example:

the words around the car	DIY words
gardening words	the vocabulary of home-buying

Variation 2

People working, but not living, in an English-speaking environment (for example, employees of British or American companies abroad, or immigrants to an English-speaking country whose home life is conducted in their mother tongue) can do very similar 'research tasks' with their colleagues, etc.

7.10 Mapping one's mood

Level **Post-beginner to advanced**

Time **15–20 minutes**

Aims **To differentiate items in a 'word field', which may easily be confused with each other, in a personal, memorable way.**

Preparation

Choose a lexical field appropriate to your students' level and cultural background. The example chosen here is *animals*, for an elementary group.

Procedure

1 Ask one student to act as secretary at the board and ask the group to brainstorm all the animal words they know. Add a few more you think they might want to learn.

2 Ask the students to work individually and write down the names of three classmates of their choice.

3 Ask each student to write down which animal/animals you, the teacher, have been like during the lesson so far, and which animal the student herself has been like. She also chooses three animals to fit the three chosen students; for example, a given student might decide she has been a goat, the teacher has been a boa constrictor, and her three classmates have been a cat, a dog, and a squirrel.

4 Group the students in fours to share the animals they have chosen for themselves and for the teacher.

5 Round off the exercise by having half a dozen people telling the group the animal they have chosen for you and why.

Variation

You can do this exercise with many sets of words, for example:

sunshine, showers, grey sky, lightning, sharp frost, monsoon, first snow
waterfall, hill, stream, moraine, plain, forest, marsh, heath, paddy field
bassoon, violin, harp, flute, cymbals, piano, triangle, piccolo

Acknowledgements

We learnt this technique from Christine Frank at Pilgrims.

7.11 A hierarchy of association

Level Intermediate to advanced
Time 20–35 minutes
Aims To organize word sets as a hierarchy.
Materials Copies of a text you or the class have chosen.

Preparation

Choose five to six key words from a text that you want them to read.

Procedure

1 Explain to the class that, when words are organized in sets, a hierarchy often emerges, representing levels of generality in the various contexts in which the words may appear. *Church*, for example, may appear high in the order in contexts such as *Church and State*, but much lower in *The Catholic church is on the corner, opposite the Baptist chapel.*

2 Before the students read the text put the first key word you have chosen on the board. With a student secretary at the board, get them to brainstorm 10–20 words they connect with the key word.

3 In a different part of your blackboard space, write up the key word on the left-hand side halfway down from the top. Ask the class which words brainstormed are of a lower level of generality, which of the same level, and which of a higher level. If the key word were *church*, here is how this board work might look:

	worship faith evil
	building religious property
church	chapel mosque temple community
	arch font crypt roof

4 Do the same with the other key words and then have the students read the text.

5 Allow time for the whole class to give feedback on how thinking about the key words before reading may have influenced their reading of the text. This can be an excellent lead-in to work on register and style.

Acknowledgements

We received the spark for this exercise from Linda Orr.

8
Personal

The best conversations are those in which the participants are motivated not only to talk but also to listen, and the best time to learn vocabulary is when the need to express or understand is at its height.

The nine activities in this chapter encourage the students to exchange more personal experiences and thoughts, including thoughts about language. 8.2, 'Life keywords', and 8.4, 'Scars', focus on experiences, while 8.8, 'Phrases I like', is more directly about language. 8.1, 'You give my talk', creates a more interactive frame for listening. 8.6, 'A letter from the teacher', introduces the vocabulary you want the class to learn in a more personal, involving way. There are other activities elsewhere in the book, such as 7.10, 'Mapping one's mood', and 11.4, 'Lexical furniture', which cover the same kind of ground.

8.1 You give my talk

Level Elementary to advanced

Time 5–10 minutes in the first class and 30–45 minutes in the second.

Aims To motivate students to listen to, and therefore learn from, each other.

Procedure

Lesson 1

1 Ask the students individually to list five topics they would like to hear a short talk on, and then in pairs to exchange lists.

2 Ask each student to choose and mark one item on their partner's list that they would be willing to talk on.

3 Students should give back the lists to their partners.

4 For homework, tell the students to prepare a vocabulary list for the topic their partner has elected to speak on.

Lesson 2

1 Have the students pair up as in the previous class and give their vocabulary lists to their partners.

2 Each student should now work individually on preparing their talk; they may use the words on their partner's list or not, as they choose, but the list will provide some idea of their future listener's knowledge of and attitude towards the subject.

3 Ask one member of each pair to give their talk to the other.

4 Ask the listener in each pair to explain how they came to construct the vocabulary list, and what they would have said in giving the same talk.

5 Repeat the activity with each listener now giving their talk.

Comments

While speakers often impose subject matter on listeners, listeners seldom have the same privilege. Here the listener suggests the topic and guides its content by proposing a set of keywords. The words chosen by the listener will also give the speaker some idea of the listener's level of knowledge of the topic: for example, given the topic 'Computers', the word-list *keyboard*, *screen*, *Microsoft*, *word processor*, *spelling* would convey a very different impression from *instruction cycle*, *run-time*, *optimize*, *kernel*, *hardware abstraction layer*.

8.2 Life keywords

Level **Elementary to advanced**

Time **25–40 minutes**

Aims **To practise and share vocabulary which is personally important.**

Procedure

1 Ask the students what date it is today. Write it on the board. Ask them what the date was seven years ago—put that on the board. Ask three or four people how old they were on that date, seven years ago.

2 Now ask the students to write down ten key emotional or idea words and phrases that sum up their lives now and a further ten to sum up their lives then.

3 Ask the students to pair off and explain the words and their significance to their partners. Have them change partners three or four times, not more, as this kind of talking is very tiring.

Examples In this activity, one person aged 39 came up with:

'Now' words	*'Past' words*
making new	change
letting free	hitch-hiking
conflict inside	shadow theatre
commitment	commitment
unease with work group	Chile
future	break with mother
retirement	
death	

Another, an 18-year-old, had:

money	marbles
university	friends
family	school
friends	music
future	father
engagement	mother

8.3 Turn out your pockets

Level **Elementary to upper-intermediate**

Time **20–35 minutes**

Aims **To use practical, day-to-day vocabulary in personally relevant conversations.**

Procedure

1 Ask each student to list some or all of the objects in their handbag/wallet/pockets: ask them to write their lists clearly.

2 When the lists are ready, ask the students to fold them and give them to you. Shuffle the lists and let each student pick one at random. No student should end up with their own list.

3 Ask the students to guess whose list they have and to tell the group why.

Acknowledgements

We learnt this exercise from Lou Spaventa. A similar one is found in G. Moskowitz. *Caring and Sharing in the Foreign Language Class.* Newbury House, 1978.

8.4 Scars

Level **Elementary to upper-intermediate**

Time **40–60 minutes**

Aims **To motivate students to overcome lack of vocabulary when narrating.**

Preparation

Bring back to mind the story of a scar you have or that a close relative of yours has.

Procedure

1 Tell the students your scar story. If it is about a scar of yours that is showable, let them see it.

2 Invite the group to think of how they got whatever scars they have. Give them a few minutes to bring their stories back to mind.

3 Ask a volunteer to tell their story. Help with words and write any accident-related vocabulary up on the board, for example, *wound, bandage, stretcher, stitches, operate.* Only write up words actually needed by the narrator.

4 Ask three or four more people to tell their scar stories to the whole group, and build up further vocabulary on the board.

5 If the class is a large one, now ask them to work in threes and continue telling scar stories, until everybody who wants to has told one.

6 Pair the students. Each student is silently to imagine a scar story for their partner. At this stage, remind them of the words on the board. Discourage them from writing.

7 Each student tells the partner the scar story they have created for them.

Variations

There are many other themes that can be used, though at different levels of intensity and involvement. If *scars* evoke short stories, for example, *hair* can produce autobiographical novels. (*How was your hair when you were eight? Can you remember the first time you visited a hairdresser's? Have you ever dyed your hair?....*)

Other themes for anecdotes that we have tried include *stairs, clothes,* and *houses.*

Comments

As we noted in the introduction, vocabulary is best learnt at the moments it is needed. Some topics are intrinsically compulsive, and will motivate the speaker to find ways of expressing their meaning despite deficiencies of vocabulary. In steps 3 and 4, the teacher has the opportunity of teaching vocabulary when the students' attention is at its height.

Acknowledgements

We learnt this exercise from Christine Frank.

8.5 Words my neighbour knows

Level Intermediate to advanced

Time 20 minutes

Aims To encourage students to teach each other and learn from each other.

Procedure

1 Divide the class into pairs.

2 Ask each student to write a list of ten words which their partner

a should know,
b should know but probably *doesn't,*
c definitely *doesn't* know.

The partners must *not* communicate at this stage.

3 Then ask the pairs to check out the accuracy of the predictions.

8.6 A letter from the teacher

Level Post-beginner to advanced

Time 10–15 minutes

Aims To present vocabulary to students in a direct, 'I–Thou' context.

Materials A copy of your letter for each student (see Preparation).

Preparation

Write a letter to your class, either about something personal you feel like telling them, about something from a previous class you want them to think back to, or about something connected with the class today. Having written the letter without thinking specially about the language add in all the synonyms you can, as in this example taken from Mario's work with an advanced class at Pilgrims:

Dear Monday Morning People,

I hope you had a good weekend, and Carmen, not too much rice
overmuch
with the host family!
homestay
How was your trip to the West Country, Celia?
excursion Devon and Cornwall
This morning I hope we will be able to interview a lady at the
woman
Students' Union, up on the UKC campus. Have you been there and
wandered across that hilltop?
strolled
Marvellous views out over the city and the gentle, orchard-covered
super/wonderful/breath-taking
hills that surround it.
are all around it /are on every side

Make a copy of your letter for each student.

Procedure

1 Give the students your letter and ask them to read it.

2 Go through those synonyms which present differences of register, for example, in the letter above *lady/woman,* and *super/wonderful.*

3 If you wish, you can comment aloud on the factors that determined *your* choice of language for *them.*

Comments

1 This is not a one-off exercise—we suggest that you use it every lesson or every week, so the students come to look forward to a letter from you. There are many techniques you can use with the letter but we feel it is enough for the students to simply read it. You may write less well than Dylan Thomas or D H Lawrence but the fact that the text is yours and uniquely written for those particular students makes it special.

2 For more activities around letters and letter-writing, see the book in this series by Nicky Burbidge et al. entitled *Letters* (1996).

3 It is much easier to pick up language from a personal letter than from a third-person text, written by and for nobody in particular.

8.7 The secret dictionary

Level Elementary to advanced

Time 15 minutes in the first lesson; 10–15 minutes in the second lesson.

Aims To express private connotations of a word or phrase—strong enough to be used as 'definitions'.

Materials A copy of the definitions texts for each student.

Preparation

Make copies of the definitions texts below, or, better, use similar texts prepared by different students in previous classes.

Procedure

Lesson 1

1 Ask the students to read 'The boy's definitions for his dog' and 'The husband's definitions for his wife'. (See below.) Point out that these have been written by the boy from the dog's point of view, and by the husband from the wife's point of view.

2 Tell them to write for homework similar definitions that encapsulate their understanding of another person's or creature's worldview. Tell them to write the definitions on detachable sheets.

Lesson 2

Ask the students to put their definitions up round the walls of the room. Ask three or four people to read theirs out.

Acknowledgements

The Devil's Dictionary (1881–1906), by Ambrose Bierce (available free online from Project Gutenberg), contains definitions such as these:

admiration, *n.* our polite recognition of another's resemblance to ourselves.
twice, *adv.* once too often.
year, *n.* a period of three hundred and sixty-five disappointments.

The boy's definitions for his dog

basket: home-place, place to arrange, place to bury bones

car: cat-cover, cat hiding-place

cat: hateful, frustrating, dangerous, potential meal

burrow: wafting spiral of scent; space to be enlarged and deepened

lamp post/wall: doggie Internet chat room

walkies: a thousand smells, tugging at the leash

The husband's definitions for his wife

children: the central task facing humans—bearers of one's hopes and ambitions

money: something necessary of which I am the recipient, similar to rain. I am not sure where either of them come from.

car: a luxury that I see as a necessity and which no one should have because of global warming

work: a general excuse that men offer to justify long absences from the reality of homelife

8.8 Phrases I like

Level **Lower-intermediate to advanced**

Time **15–25 minutes**

Aims **To encourage students to acquire a wider choice of expressions.**

Procedure

1 Group the students in threes. Tell the students each to think of three phrases they like to use when speaking English, and then to explain the phrases to their partners and tell them when they use them.

2 Each student then thinks of situations in which they could use their partners' phrases and tells their partners about them.

3 Tell each student to choose one of their own phrases and to outline three to five situations in which they would use it. They now rehearse the language for the situation *but substitute a new phrase* instead of their favourite phrase: help the students where necessary to find equivalent phrases/paraphrases.

4 Ask the students to fill the board with the substitute phrases they have found, and to teach their phrases to the rest of the class.

Comments

In our mother tongue, we show personal preference for some phrases over others. This activity asks the students (and the teacher) to extend this freedom to the target language, and at the same time to widen the range of choices made. With advanced students, this is essential in 'finding one's voice' in the other language.

8.9 What have you got ten of?

Level Beginner to lower-intermediate

Time 15–20 minutes

Aims To get students to discover and use new words to express things that are important to them now.

Procedure

1 Get a volunteer student to ask you these questions:
What have you got ten of?
What have you got three of?
Give truthful answers, for example, *ten dictionaries, three close friends.*

2 Now demonstrate the exercise the other way round, with you asking the questions up to ten. Tell the student to respond in English, but if they don't know a particular word to use their mother tongue. Put the mother-tongue word on the board, with its English equivalent.

3 Group the students in threes.

4 Round 1:
Student A asks the questions (up to ten).
Student B answers as much as possible in English.
Student C notes down any mother-tongue words B was forced to use.

5 Rounds 2 and 3: the students in the threesomes change roles and repeat the questioning.

6 Ask the 'secretary' to write on the board the mother-tongue words used in the exercise.

7 Get the class to try and find translations—if they can't, then you supply them. Rub out the mother-tongue words as the English ones replace them.

Variations

The basic question *What have you got x of?* may become limiting after a time. Here are some other productive patterns:

What three things have you got that I haven't?
What have you thrown away this week?
What five things do you wish you could do without?
If you were X, what three objects would you value most?
What things to eat could you most/least happily do without?

Comments

As we have seen in previous activities, the best time to teach vocabulary is when a student really wants to say something.

9
Word games

The activities in this chapter serve a number of purposes: they are intended to appeal to the students' puzzle-solving side; they can be used to alter the mood or focus of a lesson; and they promote experimentation. Once students have grasped the rules, most of the games can be played in 10–20 minutes, and are repeatable.

9.1 Circle games

Level Beginner to advanced

Time 10–15 minutes for each game.

Aims To provide a bank of games with a variety of learning purposes that can be played in circles of three to seven players.

Letter by letter

Player A says a letter. Player B thinks of a word beginning with A's letter and says its second letter. C thinks of a word beginning with the two letters already given and says its third letter, and so on round the circle. The person who, in saying a letter, completes a word, loses and must drop out (or lose a life). If a player, *on their turn*, thinks that the combination offered so far cannot lead to a word, they may challenge the previous player to say the word they are thinking of: if there is no such word, that player loses a life, otherwise the challenger is penalized. The game continues until only one player is left. For example:

A: d
B: o (→ dog)
C: l (→ *dole*)
D: l (→ dollar)
E: That's a word!
D loses a life.

A: c
B: h (→ change)
C: r (→ Christ)
D: o (→ chromium)
E: That's not possible: what's your word?
D: c-h-r-o-m-i-u-m
E loses a life.

Tail to head (1)

A thinks of a word and says it aloud. B has to say a word that begins with the last letter of A's word, then C a word beginning with the last letter of B's word, and so on round the circle until someone makes a mistake, or cannot find a word. (A time limit of, say, five seconds per player makes this more exciting.)

More difficult: B has to find a word beginning with the last two letters of A's word, for example:

table LEmon ONly LYmph PHarmacy ...

Tail to head (2)

A thinks of a word and says it. B has to find a word beginning with the last sound of A's word, for example:

edge join noisy evil look catch cheese ...

Theme alphabets

A chooses a category, states it, and names one member beginning with *A*, for example, *buildings: A is for Acropolis*. B must find a building beginning with *B*, for example, *B is for Bank*, and so on round the circle. ('Hard' letters such as Q and X can be omitted if wished.)

Lipograms

A chooses a letter of the alphabet and gives a short sentence which must not contain that letter. The other players, in turn, must make similar 'lipograms'.

A: 'S'. We're all in a circle.
B: It may rain tomorrow.
C: It's not raining now.
D: Wrong! There's an 'S' in 'it's'.

Sets

Find all the professions you can starting with S and ending with R (*sailor, schoolteacher, ...*). Find all the verbs of sound containing the syllable -ing- (*ring, sing, jingle, ...*).

Tonic solfa (do re mi fa so la ti do)

Round the circle, each player must make a word containing one or more of the notes of the tonic solfa, such as *do*ubt, lit*re*, co*mi*c, iso*la*te, *fa*t, p*la*ce, ins*ti*tu*ti*on.

Try exploring other areas—symbols from chemistry (re*Fe*r, *Ca*Na*da) and maths (ra*pi*d), initials and abbreviations (s*TUC*k, ra*CIA*l)—according to the background and interests of the group.

Swapped syllables

A proposes a polysyllabic word. B must change one of the syllables to make a new word, and so on round the circle, for example: contain, con*tend*, *pre*tend, pre*fer*, pre*pare*, *com*pare.

Tennis elbow foot

A says a word. Within a strict time limit (say three seconds), B must say a second word that connects with the first in some way. Then C offers a third word to connect with B's word, and so on round the circle. At any point a player may challenge the connection of another player. For example:

A: *tennis*
B: *elbow* (*tennis elbow* is an illness)
C: *foot* (*elbow* and *foot* are parts of the body)
D: *ball* (*foot* + *ball* = *football*)
E: *fall* (*fall* rhymes with *ball*)
F: *autumn* (*fall* is US synonym for *autumn*)
A: *hymn* (the last -*n* of *hymn* and *autumn* is silent)

In each group, the members decide on 'acceptable' connections.

Rhyming definitions

Each player in turn must think of a rhyming phrase and give a brief definition of it; the others must then try to guess the phrase, for example, large hog (*big pig*), happy father (*glad dad*), false pain (*fake ache*), senior policeman (*top cop*). We learnt this from Eugene Raudsepp 1977.

9.2 The prefix game

Level **Intermediate to advanced**

Time **30–40 minutes**

Aims **To work on the various negative and pejorative prefixes in English, especially for students preparing for an examination such as FCE or TOEFL.**

Preparation

Prepare a list of words and put them on the board or make a poster.

Procedure

1 Ask the students to push their books away, relax and shut their eyes. Ask them to notice their breathing. Tell them to put their fingers on one nostril while breathing in and out with the other, and then to do the same again, but swapping nostrils. (You may also choose to play calm, low-volume music in the background.)

2 With their eyes still shut, tell them you are going to read them some words. Tell them to just let the words flow over them, whether they know their meaning or not. Read these words slowly and gently:

irrational	immoral	clockwise
incapable	to misappropriate	to misbehave
serviceman	irresponsible	inaudible
incautious	illogical	disapproving
inconceivable	to apply	ex-serviceman
to function	inappropriate	intuitive
legal	unhappy	impossible
non-violent	capable	audible
logical	responsible	conceivable
unattractive	to behave	to misapply
to appropriate	to malfunction	at ease
counter-intuitive	illegal	immortal
ill-at-ease	mortal	rational

moral	anticlockwise	amoral
to pack	verbal	non-verbal
fit	to unpack	unfit

3 Read the words again twice, each time in a different order.

4 Bring two students to the board. Divide the students up into two teams, and appoint one student from each team as 'secretary'. Give team A a word that they have to make negative from the set above. Give them ten seconds' consulting time and no more. If they are right, one of the secretaries gives them a point on the board, while the other writes down the word and its negative.

5 Give team B a word to make negative, using the same procedure. Back to team A etc. …

6 At the end of the game, ask the students to jot down all the words on the board in their notebooks, adding mother-tongue translations. In a monolingual class check some of these round the class.

Variation 1

1 Put up the following on the blackboard:

in- re-
un- -tion -less
-ness -er

2 Ask the class to suggest words that contain these elements, and then to brainstorm other prefixes and suffixes.

3 Invite the students, individually or in pairs, to invent words of their own containing the brainstormed elements, and then to see if their words exist.

Variation 2

After the students have worked on a text, ask them to underline some or all of the *prefixes* and *suffixes* used, and to put a circle around all the *roots*. They should then recombine the marked elements to produce new 'words', which they can then check in their dictionaries.

Variation 3

Instead of prefixes and suffixes, you can also work with compound nouns. This is particularly useful for students whose mother tongue regularly puts adjectives after nouns, for example, French and Spanish. Even though these students may no longer make word-order mistakes with adjective + noun phrases in English, they often reverse noun + noun phrases, as *screwcork* for *corkscrew* (French *tire-bouchon*).

1 Put up the following list of nouns, or prepare your own; they are all commonly used in noun + noun combinations in English:

head	*house*	*word*	*stone*
chair	*money*	*town*	*arm*
clothes	*market*	*car*	*work*

2 Ask the students to make new words and phrases by combining pairs of words on the list or by using one word from the list and one word of their choice. Encourage them to use every word as both the first and second element in the combination, as, for example: *town hall*, *toy town*.

3 Tell them now to check the new words and phrases in a dictionary.

Comments

The relaxation exercise at the beginning can be used as an introduction to any activity demanding speed and concentration.

9.3 Definitions dictation

Level Intermediate to advanced

Time 20–30 minutes

Aims To use a guessing game to practise using definitions.

Preparation

Choose a very short text (15–20 words) and prepare definitions, hints, and clues for each of the words in it, as in the upper-intermediate example below.

Procedure

1 Explain to the students that you are going to give them a dictation, but that, instead of saying the words for them to write, you will give them definitions and clues. Ask them to work in pairs with only one person writing.

2 Dictate as follows:

You say:	The students write:
The definite article.	*The*
The word begins with *f* and means the same as *last*.	*final*
When you walk you take many of these. In the singular.	*step.*
That was the title of the poem; now for line one:	
A two-letter word that expresses doubt and ends in *f*.	*If*
Third person plural pronoun. The word ends in *y*.	*they*
Past tense of a verb with a meaning very like *do*.	*made*
Going head first into water. It ends with *ing*.	*diving*
The first word in the phrase '_ and lodging'. Here it's plural and means *planks*.	*boards*
Start a new line of the poem:	
Half a dozen.	*six*
Anglo-American units of measurement, about 2.5 centimetres long.	*inches*
The comparative form of the opposite of *long*.	*shorter*

Start a new line:

This is the verb that describes the main action of philosophers.	*think*
An anagram of WHO.	*how*
The word for *many* that you use with uncountable nouns.	*much*
The first word in the phrase '_ or later'	*sooner*

Start a new line:

Second person pronoun.	*you*
Think what trees are made of. Then think of a modal verb with the same sound. Contract it and link it to the word before with an apostrophe.	*'d*
Hamlet was worried about this infinitive.	*be*
A two-letter word. The second letter is *n*.	*in*
Definite article.	*the*
This word is wet and rhymes with *shorter*.	*water*

3 Ask one of the pairs to read out the title and the poem:

The final step

If they made diving boards
six inches shorter—
think how much sooner
you'd be in the water.

(Peter Hein. *More Grooks.* Blackwell and Mott.)

Follow-up

Once you have used this technique three or four times, ask five students, for homework, to prepare this type of dictation. Each of them dictates their definitions etc. to a fifth of the class; the five 'dictators' working simultaneously. They should keep their texts short, as in the example above.

Acknowledgements

We learnt this technique from Mitzi Powles, whose idea is quoted by Paul Rogerson in an article in the AISLI magazine, *Europa Vicina* N.6, March 2000.

9.4 Crosswords

Level Intermediate to advanced

Time No more than 20–30 minutes in any one session.

Aims To introduce students to English-language crosswords and show ways in which they can be adapted and made more creative.

Comments

Crosswords are not everyone's cup of tea, and they can be laborious and time-consuming to compose, particularly if one has to restrict oneself to common or 'useful' words. The two examples here are designed to make the teacher's, and the students', task a little easier.

Materials Copies of the crosswords for each student.

Procedure

A Anagram crosswords

Published crosswords, such as those in newspapers, can pose all sorts of problems to the non-native speaker: the words used are often obscure, the definitions may be allusive, and the cultural references may be impenetrable. One way to use them is to rewrite the definitions, or to add anagrams of the solutions as an extra help. Here is an example to get you started: add your own definitions if you wish.

Anagram Crossword

Each clue is an anagram of the word you should write in the diagram. One answer is the name of a well-known woman, now dead. Another is an English city.

Clues Across

1 THEN SCREAM
7 GAS
8 BUSH RIB
9 MEET REX
11 LAL
12 LIL
14 GRISSET
16 INDY GUN
18 OPT
19 PENNY CEDED

Clues Down

1 M TORY ISSUE
2 THING
3 RASH VET
4 BSO
5 TAVIE
6 HOLY PI SHOP
10 EGG DANE
13 DELLA
15 A TEEN
17 CEI

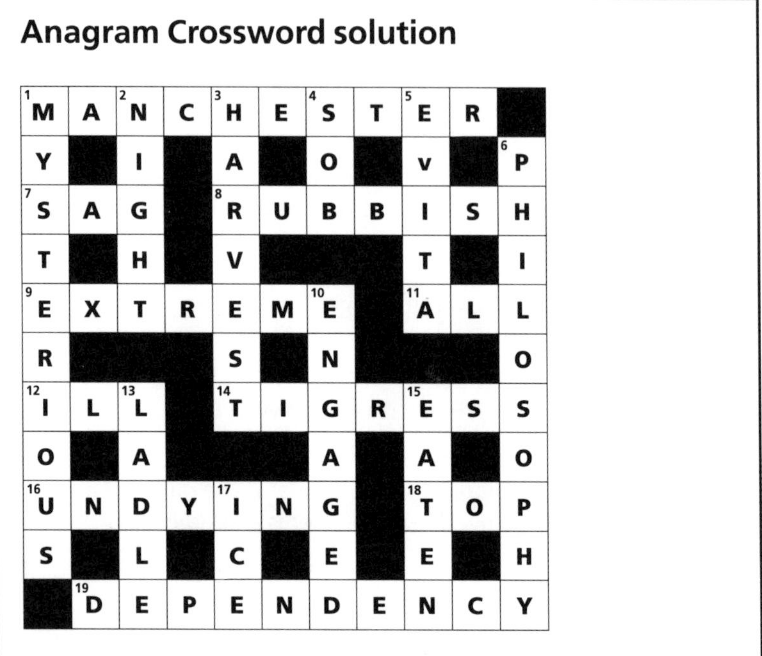

B Write your own clues

Many students find it much more fun to write the clues than to solve them. Divide the class into groups of three or four and give each group one blank diagram and one completed diagram and one or more dictionaries. Tell the groups to choose a secretary and to compose clues for the crossword, which the secretary should write under the blank diagram. When they have finished, the groups should exchange the blank diagrams and clues and try to solve the puzzles.

Here are four completed diagrams and four blank diagrams to start with:

1 V	E	2 R	B		3 A	4 B	L	5 E
E		E		6 S		R		V
7 A	D	J	E	C	T	I	V	E
L		E		A		L		N
	8 A	C	U	T	E	L	Y	
9 S		T		T		I		10 S
11 W	H	I	T	E	W	A	S	H
A		O		R		N		I
12 N	I	N	E		13 S	T	O	P

C Software aids to crossword setting and solving

There are several programs available to assist in designing and printing diagrams. Our favourite is Henry Casson's *Crossword Utility*, downloadable free from http://home.freeuk.net/dharrison/puzzles/utility.htm.

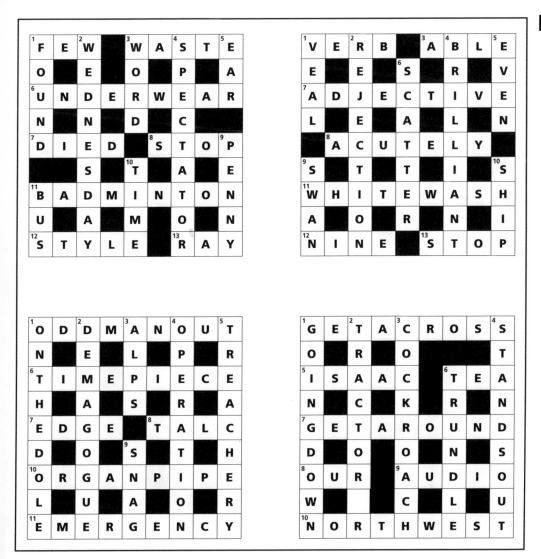

There are also programs to assist in finding words to fit into your diagram: you can choose your own words, or ask the program to search a word list for words that will fit. More than one word list (or phrase list) can be used, and you can write your own lists, or make

9.4

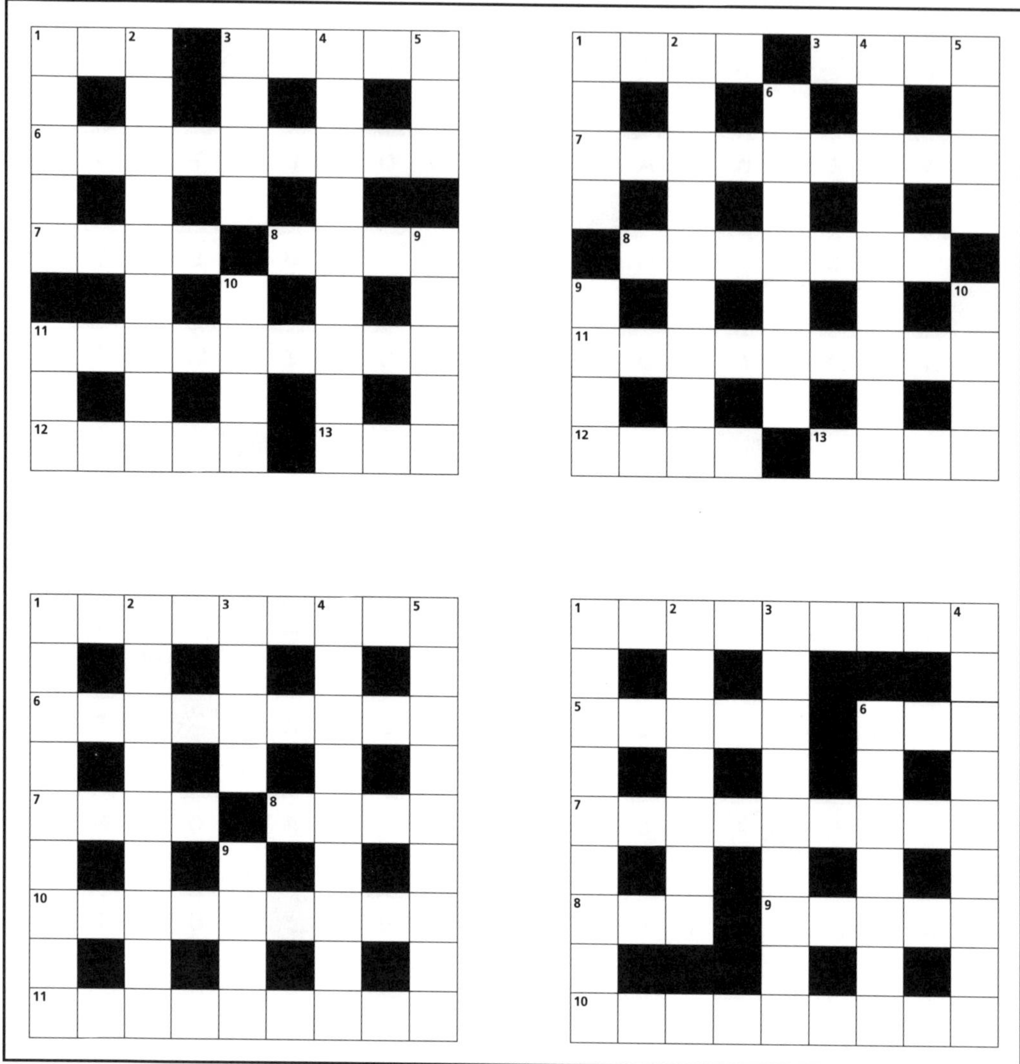

Photocopiable © John Morgan

one from a corpus of texts using concordance software. (See Chapter 5.) Good examples are *TEA & Sympathy* from http://bryson.ltd.uk and *Crossword Compiler 6* from http://www.crossword-puzzle-maker.com.

Finally, students (and teachers) interested in looking at how 'cryptic' puzzles work will get a lot of help from the surprisingly effective crossword-solving program *Crossword Maestro*, from http://www.genius2000.com.

9.5 Pivot words

Level **Lower-intermediate to advanced**
(The example here is upper-intermediate.)

Time **20–30 minutes**

Aims **To explore the different semantic and grammatical uses of words.**

Materials **One copy of a worksheet for each student (optional).**

Preparation

Collect together 10–20 'double sentences' (see below) at a level appropriate for your class, type them out, and make copies.

Procedure

1 Write this example up on the board:

Who is the Prime Minister of this ***country*** *hotels are nice to stay in, aren't they?*

Show the students how ***country*** is a pivot word. It is the last word of the first sentence and the first word of the second sentence:

Who is the Prime Minister of this ***country?***
Country *hotels are nice to stay in, aren't they?*

Explain that you are going to give the students a dictation of 'double' sentences like the one above. They are to take down your words and underline the pivot word. Point out that in two of the examples the 'pivot word' will have two different spellings.

2 Dictate these ten 'double sentences':

Old people need quite a lot of help me down these steps, would you?
Babies can keep you awake at night watchmen keep the neighbourhood safe.
Small kids love a rough and tumble driers are useful in winter.
They decided to shear the ewe really need a haircut.
Husbands are often late husbands can be a matter of regret.
He took his clothes off-the-cuff speeches are hard to make.
Mary had a little lamb stew is on the menu for lunch today.
The old woman lived in an expensive house prices have gone up recently.
Home is the place to come back to and two make four.
Our team won the game pie is really delicious.

3 Pair the students so they can compare their answers.

4 Ask students round the class to read out the 20 sentences.

5 For homework ask them to come to class with six double sentences each.

6 In the next class, group the students in fours to work on each other's sentences.

Variation 1

You can use this technique to focus on phrasal verbs, for example:

Never give ***up*** *the mountain they went.*

I'm afraid you let me ***down*** *the road and then right and then you're there.*

or on differences of spelling, for example:

Add some rosemary and ***time*** *travel is impossible.* (**thyme**)

or on features of pronunciation, for example, liaison in

If I see a mouse, ***I scream*** *comes in many flavours.* (**ice cream**)

(For US speakers, and some UK speakers, there is also a difference in stress here.)

Variation 2

A development of the above is to present the 'double sentences' with the pivot words omitted. This is more difficult, but appeals to a puzzle mentality.

Acknowledgements

This idea comes from Milton Erickson's work with hypnotic language patterns.

9.6 Hiding words

Level Lower-intermediate to advanced

Time 10–20 minutes

Aims To discover words 'buried' in other words or surrounding text.

Materials Dictionaries.

Procedure

1 Put up the following words on the board:

THE CENT

Explain that many words can be found hidden inside other words:

oTHEr reCENTly

and even inside phrases:

I took the BUS Home. Do you knoW HER E-mail address?

2 Put on the board, or ask the students to select, three to five words. Ask the students to hide them, one or more to a sentence, as in the examples you gave. Tell them they can use dictionaries to find the words for their sentences, but not to spend too long on this: if they cannot easily find a way to 'hide' a word, they should discard it and move on to another.

3 Get the students to exchange their sentences and find their partner's hidden words.

Variation 1

Hide the words as every other letter of the new word or phrase, for example:

PIGEON → my speed kept sliPpInG bElOw Ninety kilometres an hour.

Variation 2

Hide the words backwards:

KNIT → sTINKing fish

Variation 3

Use each letter of the word as the first letters of the words of a phrase:

TEACH → Take Everything And Come Home

Comments

1 Games like this appeal to lovers of logical puzzles, intelligence tests, crossword puzzles, and so on. Many students will prefer constructing the contexts to finding the hidden words.

2 Students may be weak in English, but strong in puzzle-solving, and vice versa. As a help to those who cannot spot the hidden word, add a brief definition.

9.7 Treasure hunt

Level **Intermediate to advanced**

Time **10–20 minutes, or as homework.**

Aims **To practise identifying words with the help of definitions.**

Preparation

Make a 'word chain' like that shown below, in which each word overlaps its neighbours by exactly three letters. You will find some more example wordchains at the end of this activity.

Write a simple definition for each word in the chain and put the definitions and the number of letters in each word on a worksheet, as in the example below. To get the students started, give the first three letters of the first word.

Procedure

1 Write on the board the following string of letters:

PRACTICALENDARTBOARDENTERRIBLEACHIEVENING

2 Using coloured chalk or markers, or by underlining, show that this is a wordchain in which each word overlaps its neighbours by exactly three letters:

PRACTI CAL EN DAR TBO ARD EN TER RI BLE ACH I EVE NING

3 Give out the worksheet and let the students get on with it. The exercise can be done individually, in pairs or small groups, or as homework.

4 Students should also be encouraged to prepare worksheets for each other.

Comments

As in a treasure hunt, each question has to be answered before the next can be attempted. This can be frustrating for some people!

Example worksheet

1 n. representative of a group or category
EXA _ _ _ _ (7)

2 adj. enjoyable _ _ _ _ _ _ _ _ (8)

3 adj. very old _ _ _ _ _ _ _ (7)

4 adj. feeling sick (in the stomach) _ _ _ _ _ _ (6)

5 n. protection given by a state to a political refugee
_ _ _ _ _ _ (6)

6 n. timber, wood for building _ _ _ _ _ _ (6)

7 adj. lacking, esp. in hope or support _ _ _ _ _ _ (6)

Key

EXAMPLEASANTIQUEASYLUMBEREFT

Suggested wordchains

Here are some more word chains from which you (or your students) can prepare your own worksheets:

BURDENTALISMANAGERMANYHOWEVERDICTIONARY

AROUNDERNEATHENSIGNPOSTEOPATHYROID

TIPSYCHIATRICKSHAWTHORNAMENTIRETYMOLOGY

ARMCHAIRBRUSHERMITTENTACLEVERBATIMIDRIFFY

INGOTHICCUPBOARDOURSELVESTRYING

(The last one is a word necklace!)

9.8 Storyboard

Level Elementary to advanced

Time 20–30 minutes

Aims To practise relating words to context.

Materials Word cards (see Preparation).

Preparation

Choose a short text, preferably containing not too much new lexical material for the class. Write it out clearly on cards measuring 20 × 15 cm, one word to a card, so that each word is clearly visible to the whole class. On the back of each card write the same word very small.

Procedure

1 Stick the cards to the wall or blackboard in the correct text sequence, with the large-print side hidden.

2 Tell the class that there is a text on the blackboard which they will have to uncover, one word at a time. Ask them to shout out any words that come to mind: if you hear any of the words in the text, reverse the corresponding card immediately, using the small-print words as a reminder.

3 From chance beginnings, the text will gradually appear, as more and more context becomes available to the students.

Variation

If you can memorize a short text exactly, then you can of course dispense with the cards on the blackboard. Short poems, especially ones with clear rhyme and rhythm, are ideal for this.

Comments

This was originally devised as a computer game, but, with a little preparation by the teacher, works even better on the blackboard.

Acknowledgements

John Higgins and Graham Davies. *Storyboard.* Wida Software, 1982.

10
Dictionary exercises and word history

The first three activities in this chapter aim to familiarize students with dictionaries and show how to use them in enjoyable, creative ways. 10.4, 'What do I mean?', looks at the language we need to explain and comment on how we use words, and 10.8, 'Thesauri', shows how a thesaurus can be used to stimulate thought and discussion. 10.5, 'Borrowed words', and the two activities that follow cater for students who are interested in the history of words.

The choice of which dictionary to use depends very much on the students' level, interests and learning style. New dictionaries are also constantly appearing, which makes it hard to give concrete recommendations.

Jon Wright's *Dictionaries*, in this series (1998), contains a number of very useful suggestions for choosing, using, and finding your way round dictionaries.

10.1 Word dip

Level Elementary to advanced

Time 15–25 minutes

Aims To familiarize students with the structure, uses, and limitations of dictionaries.

Materials Sufficient monolingual dictionaries to have one for each group of two to four students. Any monolingual dictionary will do, though for more advanced students the various learners' dictionaries may be less stimulating. Pocket dictionaries will not be adequate.

Procedure

1 Ask the students to form groups of 3–5 players each. Make sure each group has a dictionary.

2 Explain or demonstrate the game, then ask the groups to play one complete round. The game goes like this:

a Player A opens the dictionary at random.

b A chooses a word defined on the pages open and tells the other players what it is: this may be a word A thinks the other players do not know, or a known word which has a less well-known meaning, such as *found* (= *establish*, as well as being the past tense of *find*). It may be helpful to insist that A both pronounces the word and spells it out. A may also give other information, such as part of speech, but not meaning.

c The other players then question A on the meaning (or the specific meaning chosen by A) of the word. A may only answer *yes* or *no*.

d A scores a point if no one guesses the meaning within, say, 20 questions. Otherwise the first person to guess the meaning gets the point.

Two or three rounds should be the maximum to sustain interest. If the students wish to continue, then repeat the game on a later occasion.

10.2 From word to word

Level **Intermediate to advanced**

Time **15–25 minutes**

Aims **To give further practice in the use of dictionaries, with the emphasis on the language used in the definitions given.**

Materials **Sufficient monolingual dictionaries to have one for each student. It will be more interesting if you provide a selection of different dictionaries.**

Procedure

1. Ask the students to work individually. Give each student a dictionary, or make sure they have brought one to class.
2. Write up a word on the blackboard. Choose one which will produce a rich set of paraphrases/synonyms.
3. Ask the students to look up in the dictionary the word you have put on the board and to read through the definition(s). Then ask them to choose one of the words in the definition and to look that up.
4. Ask the students to continue in this way until they have looked up, say, a dozen words. At each stage they should write down the word they look up.
5. Ask them to form pairs and compare their lists.

Example Starting from the headword plant, one person produced this list:

plant → *vegetable* → *organism* → *structure* → *framework* → *skeleton* → *bone* → *bobbin* → *reel* → *cylinder* → *tubular* → chamber

and another:

plant → *grow* → *increase* → *rise* → *swell* → *waves* → *hair* → *thread* → *cotton* → understand

Variation

Students who share the same mother tongue can do the exercise using a good bilingual dictionary, moving back and forth between English and mother-tongue entries.

Follow-up 1

After working through steps 1–4 above, ask the students to link the words in their list into a paragraph or short story.

Follow-up 2

Ask the students to use the technique above to 'quarry' words relating to a particular subject or theme (for example, words needed in writing a description, words used by policemen).

10.3 Write yourself in

Level Elementary to advanced

Time 10–15 minutes

Aims To add a strong personal element to dictionary practice.

Materials Dictionaries.

Preparation

Select 6–12 words from a text or other source of vocabulary.

Procedure

1. Ask the students, working individually, to look up each of the selected words in their dictionary. When they have read the entry and any example sentences given, they should construct an example sentence for that word including their own name, or a reference to themselves. So, if a student were to look up *take one's mind off* and find the example *Hard work always takes your mind off domestic problems*, they might write *English classes take my mind off work.*
2. In small groups, the students compare their example sentences.

Variation

This exercise can easily be adapted as a pair exercise by asking the pairs to write sentences that apply to both members, for example:

veal: We are both opposed to the production of white veal.

10.4 What do I mean?

Level Lower-intermediate to advanced

Time 10–15 minutes in the first class; 10–20 minutes in later classes.

Aims To introduce and practise words and phrases used in defining and explaining meanings.

Procedure

Lesson 1

1 Invite one student to ask you a question in front of the class. Instead of answering immediately, pick out a word or phrase from their question and put a question back to them, for example,

Student: *What's your favourite colour?*
Teacher: *What do you mean by 'favourite colour'?*
Student: *The colour you like to wear.*
Teacher: *In that case, my favourite colour is blue.*

2 Ask the students to form pairs and to put questions back and forth to each other in the way you have shown.

3 After five minutes, tell them to take a piece of paper and, working individually, to recall two or three of the questions they were asked. They should then write their answers as single sentences including the phrase *by which I mean*, for example:

My favourite colour, by which I mean the colour I like to wear, is blue.

Lesson 2

1 Remind the class of the previous activity by writing your original example sentence on the board, underlining the phrase *by which I mean:*

My favourite colour, by which I mean the colour I like to wear, is blue.

2 Teach, or get the class to brainstorm, other phrases that can be used instead of *by which I mean*, for example:

in other words	that is (to say)	in the sense of
or rather	meaning	i.e.

3 Tell the students to rewrite a short text by picking out as many words and phrases from it as they want and adding to each a comment introduced by one of the phrases in the above list. See the example below.

Example text Country people have a different attitude to the road from town people. They are not better drivers, but they are more considerate.

Example text rewritten Country people, that is people who both live and work in the countryside, have a different attitude to the road from town people. They are not better, in the sense of technically more competent, drivers, but they are more considerate. By this I mean they actually consider what they, and other drivers, are doing while they drive along.

Follow-up

Use the questioning and rewrite techniques to explore other ways in which we seek to clarify, modify, comment on, or correct the language we are using. Here are a few example sets of phrases:

a clarifying by example:

for example	for instance	..., say, ...
Take ...		

b specifying:

in particular	specifically	particularly
to be specific	to name one	

c approximating:

in a sense	more or less	in a manner of speaking
sort of	as it were	to an extent
for want of a better word		

d abandoning an explanation or example:

etc.	and so on
and so forth	you know what I mean
you know the sort of thing I mean	work it out for yourself

Comments

The dictionary is not the only place where definitions are found. We are constantly explaining, paraphrasing, and commenting on the meaning of the words we use. Here the student is encouraged to learn some of the words we need in order to talk about words.

10.5 Borrowed words

Level Intermediate to advanced

Time 20 minutes

Aims To show how words can change form and meaning across languages.

Materials Copies of the word list and key for each student.

Preparation

Prepare a set of English words that derive from words in other languages: if your class contains speakers of different mother tongues, try to represent each of these languages in your set. Put the whole list on a sheet of paper and make a copy for each member of the class. An example set is given below.

Procedure

1 Give out the word lists. Tell the students which original languages are represented by the words and ask them, working individually, to match them to the words in the list.

2 The students may now compare and discuss their answers. This is particularly useful if you have included words borrowed from languages spoken by the students.

3 Give out the key. Ask the students to check their answers not only against the key but also in a dictionary. They should pay attention to the pronunciation (which may be very different from that in the original language), the meaning(s) (which may well have changed or become restricted), and, if the dictionary also gives etymologies (for example, *OED*, *Chambers*), something of the *how*, *when*, and even *why* of the borrowing. (In the example list below, *tea* was borrowed from Cantonese, not Mandarin; *pork* refers to the meat of the pig, not to the animal itself; *sherry* derives from an older pronunciation of Spanish *Jerez*; *bungalow* came from a Hindi word that simply means 'of Bengal'.)

Word list

ginseng	tea	soya	alcohol
pundit	typhoon	decide	atmosphere
hippopotamus	siesta	curry	torso
lute	cattle	orange	chemist
atom	opera	coolie	pork
bungalow	canasta	kilogram	apron
marzipan	sherry	armada	piano

Key

Arabic	Spanish	Indian languages	French	Italian	Chinese	Greek
alcohol	siesta	bungalow	apron	torso	typhoon	atmosphere
lute	canasta	curry	pork	marzipan	tea	hippopotamus
orange	sherry	pundit	cattle	opera	soya	kilogram
chemist	armada	coolie	decide	piano	ginseng	atom

10.6 Commemorative words

Level Upper-intermediate to advanced

Time 20–30 minutes

Aims To explore words with a history.

Materials Etymological and other dictionaries.

Preparation

Take several etymological dictionaries to class. You may also like to read up a little on the people and events referred to.

Procedure

1 Get a secretary to come to the board and then dictate these words to them:

sandwich	*wellingtons*	*spa*
plimsoll	*quisling*	*hoover*
mackintosh	*biro*	*caesarian*
volcano	*quixotic*	*meander*
marathon	*to meet your Waterloo*	
cardigan	*to cross the Rubicon*	

2 Check that all the words are semantically known to the students, especially harder ones like *plimsoll*: found in the phrase *plimsoll line*, the safe loading line on a ship; also a type of sports footwear.

3 Explain that all the words or phrases refer back to the name of a person, a place, or an event. Ask them if they can identify any of these.

4 Ask the students to work in small groups and give each group a dictionary. Assign a small group of words to each group of students.

5 Ask the groups to look up their words and find the person, place or event that lies behind each.

6 Each group teaches the whole class the derivation of their words.

10.7 Dating words

Level Upper-intermediate to advanced

Time 15–30 minutes

Aims To explore more words with a history, with the emphasis on more recent coinages.

Materials A copy of the wordlist for each student.

Preparation

Make a list of words that you are confident most of the class are familiar with, or use the example list given below (with the years omitted). Include as many recently introduced words/meanings as you can. Make enough copies for each student or group of students.

Procedure

1 Ask the students to work either alone or in groups of two to three.

2 Give out one copy of the wordlist to each student or group.

3 Ask the students to write next to each word the approximate year when it was first used in English.

4 Get the students/groups to join together to compare their answers. Ask them to check their answers against an appropriate dictionary, or give out the example list again with the dates included. For newer words, we recommend John Ayto's *Twentieth-Century Words* (1999) and

Elizabeth Knowles' *Oxford Dictionary of New Words* (1997). For older words, the *Oxford English Dictionary* (Second edition) gives dated citations of almost every word defined.

Word list

poverty line (1901)	green = ecological (1972)	car bomb (1972)
nappy (1927)	crew-cut (1940)	jingle (noun) (1930)
think-tank (1959)	carer (1978)	sitcom (1964)
pylon (1923)	drop-out (1930)	genocide (1944)
fab (1957)	gremlin (1941)	in-house (1956)
doodle (1937)	rock and roll (1954)	cassette (1960)

Here is an example entry from John Ayto's excellent *Twentieth-Century Words*:

fab *adj* (1957) wonderful, marvellous. Slang. A shortening of fabulous (which is not recorded in print in this sense until 1959). The usage really took off around 1963, when it became attached to the Beatles (sometimes called 'The Fab Four') and other Merseyside pop groups. After lying dormant for a while, it enjoyed a revival in the 1980s (see **fabbo** (1984)).
1963 *Times*. She stretched her stockinged toes towards the blazing logs. 'Daddy, this fire's simply fab.'
1963 *Meet the Beatles*. Most of the Merseyside groups produce sounds which are pretty fab.
1988 *National Lampoon*: 'And I just think it's fab!'

To which we should add that *fab* is now back in a period of 'dormancy'.

10.8 Thesauri

Level **Upper-intermediate to advanced**

Time **30–45 minutes**

Aims **To show how words may be grouped by meaning and context; to introduce and practise using a thesaurus; and, incidentally, to show how words can be used to disguise and distort meaning.**

Materials **Dictionaries, copies of the Thesaurus extract and worksheet**

Preparation

Choose a word or phrase with strong or controversial associations. Make an extract from a thesaurus entry containing it, or use the example below, and prepare enough copies for each student to have one. You should also make copies of the worksheet (which can be used with any item chosen) for everyone. Provide a variety of dictionaries and other reference books in class.

Procedure

1 Write the word or phrase (in this case the word *terrorist*) in the centre of the board, then get five to ten students (depending on the size of your class and of the board) to write all the words and phrases they can think of that have the same, or a similar, meaning. Tell them to scatter the words around the board, not in neat rows and columns, and stop them after two minutes.

2 When all the students are back in their seats, tell them to take a piece of paper and copy down the words on the board, arranging them into groups according to meaning. Tell them that they may also add any other words of similar meaning that come into their minds, but are not on the board.

3 Tell the students to stand up, walk around, and compare what they have written. Keep them moving round: in a class of 20, every student should have read what at least eight others have written after ten minutes.

4 Give out copies of the Thesaurus extract and ask them to look through it. Tell them what a thesaurus is (a collection of words, arranged in groups according to meaning, but without definitions or examples), and that it can be a useful aid to memory and imagination. Stress that it is not a 'collection of synonyms', and that to get best value out of it, one should use it in conjunction with a dictionary.

5 Give every student a copy of the Worksheet. Tell them they have 15 minutes to complete it. Encourage them to use dictionaries and reference books, and to ask you and each other questions.

6 Group the students in fours to compare and discuss what they have done.

Worksheet

1 Look through the Thesaurus extract, underlining any words and phrases you have not met before, or which you would like to learn more about.

2 Choose five of the words or phrases you have underlined, look them up in the dictionary, and write an example sentence for each:

_______________ : _______________

_______________ : _______________

_______________ : _______________

_______________ : _______________

_______________ : _______________

3 Look through the extract again. Which two words or phrases are for you most alike in meaning? Write them here:

_______________ _______________

4 Which two words or phrases are most different in meaning?

_______________ _______________

5 Write down five words or phrases which you would be surprised to find in the same short text (essay, newspaper article, radio talk, short story, etc.).

_______________ _______________ _______________

_______________ _______________

6 Write down five words or phrases which are not in the extract, but ought to be.

_______________ _______________ _______________

_______________ _______________

7 Which single word or phrase in the extract is closest in meaning to the one printed in **bold text**?

____

8 And which is furthest in meaning from that word or phrase?

____

10.8

Thesaurus extract

#361. [Destruction of life; violent death.] Killing.—
N. killing &c. v.; homicide, manslaughter, murder, assassination; blood, bloodshed; gore, slaughter, carnage, butchery; massacre; fusillade, pogrom, thuggery, Thuggism [obs].
deathblow, finishing stroke, coup de grace, quietus; execution &c.
(capital punishment) 972; judicial murder; martyrdom.
butcher, slayer, murderer, Cain, assassin, **terrorist**, cutthroat, hitman, thug, racketeer, gunman, matador; gallows, executioner &c. (punishment) 975; man-eater, apache[obs], hatchet man.
regicide, parricide, matricide, fratricide, infanticide, foeticide[obs], uxoricide[obs].
suicide, felo de se[obs], hara-kiri, suttee; immolation, auto da fe, holocaust.
suffocation, strangulation, garrotte; hanging &c. v. deadly weapon &c. (arms) 727; [. . .]

#913. [Maleficent being] Evil doer — N. evil doer; wrongdoer &c. 949; mischief-maker; oppressor, tyrant; destroyer, Vandal; iconoclast.
firebrand, incendiary, firebug [U.S.], pyromaniac; anarchist, communist, **terrorist**.
savage, brute, ruffian, barbarian, caitiff [obs], desperado; Apache[obs], hoodlum, hood, plug-ugly, pug-ugly [U.S.], tough [U.S.]; Mohawk; bully, rough, hooligan, larrikin[Aus], ugly customer; thief &c. 792.
cockatrice, scorpion, hornet.
snake, viper, adder, snake in the grass; serpent, cobra, asp, rattlesnake.
cannibal; anthropophagus, anthropophagist; bloodsucker, vampire, ogre, ghoul, gorilla, vulture.
wild beast, tiger, hyena, butcher, hangman; blood-hound, hell-hound.
hag, beldam, Jezebel.
monster; fiend &c. (demon) 980; devil incarnate, demon in human form; Frankenstein's monster.
harpy, siren; Furies, Eumenides.
Hun, Attila, scourge of the human race.[. . .]

A note on Roget's Thesaurus

Roget's original *Thesaurus of English Words and Phrases* has long been out of copyright. Now there are innumerable versions all claiming to be Roget's Thesaurus, and all independently copyrighted. These differ in many ways: some are based on British, others on American English; some are highly literary, while others are based on up-to-date spoken English. Most follow Roget's original plan, as in the extract opposite, but there are also 'alphabetical thesauri' such as that published by Oxford University Press, and electronic versions that can be used with your word-processor.

The full text of the 1911 edition is available from the web: you can find it by visiting http://www.gutenberg.net. When you have downloaded the file (about 1.5Mb), you can open it in your word-processor and search for what you need. (The **Thesaurus extract** opposite is taken from this public-domain version.)

There are also online versions, which enable you to type in a search word or phrase and receive an HTML page containing the appropriate section(s) of *Roget*. One of these can be found at http://www.bartleby.com/thesauri .

Other online thesauri

1 Plumb Design's *Visual Thesaurus* at http://www.visualthesaurus.com is a remarkable combination of thesaurus and mind-map. When you enter a word, a graphics display opens with your word in the centre, joined to other words of similar meaning by spidery lines. If you click on any of these, the display changes to make the new word central, and other words appear or are replaced. To use it, you will need to enable Java in your browser.

2 The *Lexical FreeNet* thesaurus at http://www.lexfn.com allows a search on one word (in which case it gives a list of synonyms) or on a pair of words. If you enter two words, it will return a series of words linking the first to the second. For example, *dream* and *leviathan* yield:

dream → *nightmare* → *horror* → *monster* → *leviathan*

11
Revision exercises

Traditionally, revision has been much more on teachers' maps than other aspects of vocabulary work. A colleague in Cambridge started each morning on her intensive courses by asking students to close their eyes and think back over what they learnt the previous day. Examinations, the curriculum, and the teacher's human need to believe that she has actually *taught* the students something, all encourage the use of revision exercises, but we believe that there is a deeper need: one simply does not 'learn' something by encountering it once. With vocabulary, students need to meet, and use, and reflect on words many times, in different contexts and settings, in the company of different people, and, perhaps, in different frames of mind, before they can be said to have truly learnt a word or phrase.

A note on notebooks

Many of the exercises that follow should be done in the students' vocabulary notebooks. In this way learners will have a powerful record of the exercises they have done with and around new lexis. Many activities here aim, for example, to improve the *visual quality* of notebooks, to go beyond the monotonous column of bilingual pairs:

Frau – woman
und – and
Stuhl – chair

A ground plan of one's home with the words you were learning written all over it is a lot more memorable than this. (See 11.4, 'Lexical furniture'.)

The vocabulary notebook may well be a sort of history of the language class: students can write personal notes about the circumstances of learning as well as the apparent 'content' of the lesson. From a Greek student, for example, we might have the following page:

ghost (phantasma)	Got a good letter from home today.
conviction (pepithesis)	The teacher is looking out of the window.
politics	It's a Greek word—I got the English stress wrong again!
metaphor	Makes me think of moving house.

11.1 Open categorization

Level Beginner to advanced

Time 15–20 minutes

Aims To allow students to categorize vocabulary in any way they want.

Procedure

1 Write the words to be reviewed on the board.

2 Invite the students, working individually, to categorize the words into more than two groups. The way they do this is up to them: the look of the words on the page, associations with the words, the sound of the words, idea groupings, etc. Do not tell the students how to categorize: let them find out for themselves.

3 Ask the students to give each of their categories a heading.

4 Go round the class asking some of the students to read out their headings and the words in the corresponding categories. Do not reward or censure students by your facial expression and tone of voice for the way they have categorized: be as neutral as you can and say as little as possible. How the students group the words is up to them, and telling them that they are 'right' or 'wrong' will only increase their dependence on you.

Comments

If you are working with beginners, they will use their mother tongue.

Acknowledgements

We learnt this technique from Caleb Gattegno's *Silent Way*. For more about his work, and especially his views on learner independence and the role of the teacher, see his book, *The Common Sense of Teaching Foreign Languages*. Educational Solutions, 1976.

11.2 Guided categorization

Level Beginner to advanced

Time 15–20 minutes

Aims To get the students to form interesting and memorable word groups, and to deepen their understanding of words by comparing categorizations.

Procedure

A Nice words versus nasty words

1 Give the students the words to be reviewed and ask them each to pick three they like and three they don't. Give them time to think.

2 Put up two headings on the board: *Nice words* and *Nasty words*. Ask each student to write up *one* of their nice words and *one* nasty word.

3 When everybody has two words on the board, invite people to explain why they like or dislike particular words. Do not gloss or comment yourself: don't give or withhold approval. By keeping quiet you will help the students to talk.

Example In one group the review words were:

viaduct	ambulance	to lower	motorway
plunge	jack-knife	to volunteer	hair-raising
jelly	windscreen	intensive	

Here are some of the things different students said about some of the words:

ambulance	*I used to be a nurse and an ambulance coming meant more work. I don't like the word.*
intensive	*I don't like it because the -nt- is too hard to say correctly.*
jelly	*I like it. The sound is right.*
windscreen	*I don't like it because I learnt it last term and can't remember it.*

Variation

The exercise above can be adapted to run over the course of a whole term:

1 Get a large sheet of card to hang on your classroom wall. Find a closed box and make a slot in the top: these will become permanent classroom fixtures.

2 Invite students to stick on the large sheet any words they like, or that interest them. These may be single words written on slips of paper, cuttings from newspaper headlines or advertisements, etc. Ask them to 'throw away' in the box any words they don't like, or can't or don't want to remember, or which confuse or bother them. Tell them they can do this whenever they like during the course.

3 From time to time, hold comment sessions: let the students introduce their own words first, followed by comments from others. Try to keep in the background and let the students run their own session.

B Other binary subjective categories

Using the methodology suggested in **A**, you can ask the students to work on contrastive categories of many different sorts, for example,

very English words	not very English words
new words	old words
me-connected words	separate-from-me words
high words	low words
past words	future words

C Words and shapes

1 Put up on the board the following shapes:

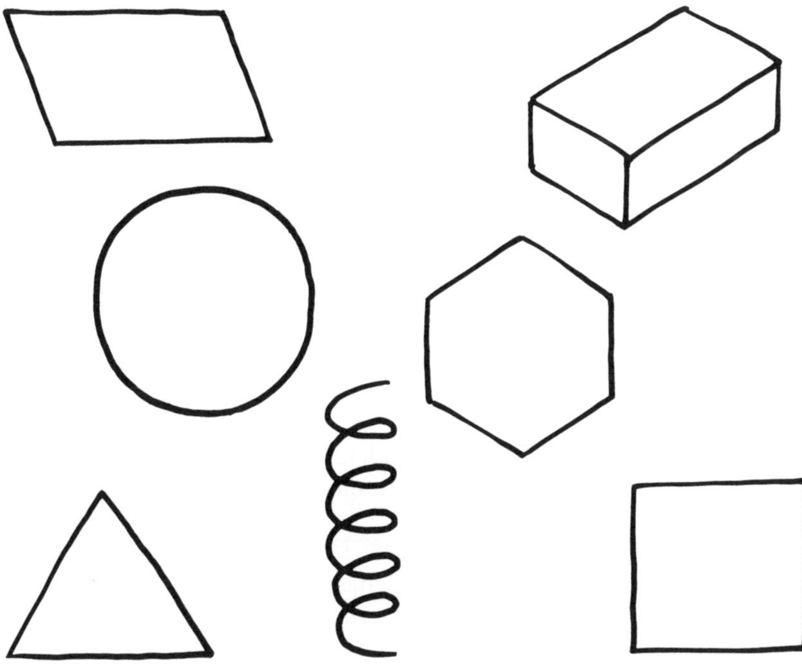

2 Ask the students to copy the shapes into their notebooks and then associate the words to be reviewed with the shapes. They may, of course, link a given word with more than one shape.

3 Pair the students and let them explain their word-shape associations.

D Words and countries

1 Ask the students to jot down the name of a country they have enjoyed visiting or would like to visit.

2 Have them draw maps of these countries on the blackboard. (Inaccuracy gives life to the exercise.)

3 Ask them to write down the names of the various countries across the top of a piece of paper, and then to rule the paper into columns, each with a country as a heading.

4 Put up your list of words and ask the students to write them in one or other column according to the associations they feel between their words and the countries.

5 Ask them to explain their associations to their neighbours.

Example In one class the list of words under review was:

shed	translucent	corrugated	hefty	staple
loop	rack	hinge	hook	lethal
draughty	pail	suck	drain	goat

One student produced these associations:

Romania	Mongolia	Denmark	Wales	USA	Tanzania
shed pail suck goat	translucent	hinge rack		lethal drain hefty	draughty corrugated
No associations: staple/loop/hook					

E Words and colours

1 Ask each student to write down six colours in order of preference ranging from most liked to most disliked. (For this exercise black and white are colours.)

2 Put a set of words on the board and ask the students to associate the words with the colours. They should do this individually in writing.

3 Ask individual students to tell the group which colours they assigned to different words and why.

Acknowledgements

We should like to thank Marilyn Spaventa, who used this technique with classes on Pilgrims summer courses.

11.3 Words on a scale

Level **Intermediate to advanced**

Time **15–20 minutes**

Aims **To concentrate the students' attention on the words under revision by focusing on their own, subjective reactions.**

Procedure

1 Put the table below up on the board. Explain that it shows a series of scales between extremes, and ask the students to copy it into their notebooks:

valuable — — — — worthless
shallow — — — — deep
slow — — — — fast
active — — — — passive
small — — — — large
clean — — — — dirty
weak — — — — strong
tasty — — — — distasteful
relaxed — — — — tense
cold — — — — hot

2 Write the words to be revised on another part of the board and ask the students, working individually, to choose six words and decide where each of them should go on each scale. If one of the words to be revised were *consistency*, for example, a student's scales might look like this:

valuable _X_ ___ ___ ___ ___ *worthless*
shallow ___ ___ ___ _X_ ___ *deep*
slow ___ ___ _X_ ___ ___ *fast*
active ___ _X_ ___ ___ ___ *passive*

This student thinks *consistency* is a valuable quality that probably indicates depth. Speed seems unimportant but it takes an active stance to be consistent.

3 Pair the students and ask them to explain their scales to a partner.

11.4 Lexical furniture

Level **Elementary to advanced**

Time **15–20 minutes**

Aims **To fix vocabulary in memory by visualizing connections with familiar objects and places.**

Procedure

1 Ask each student to draw a ground plan of their house/flat/home/room.

2 Put up on the blackboard a set of twenty or so words for revision.

3 Working on their own, the students should then place the words in appropriate positions in their living place.

4 In pairs, they look at each others' placings and discuss them.

Example In one class, a girl put *perplexed* in the garage because her mother could never understand why her car would not start. She put *furious* outside the house because her parents would not allow expressions of anger inside, and *do an experiment* in the kitchen.

Variation 1

Each student draws a clockface: the words to be reviewed are placed on the clockface according to temporal associations.

Variation 2

Ask the students to write down twenty times of day when regular things happen, for example:

8.15 Wife leaves for work.
8.30 Postman comes.
9.10 I finish washing up the breakfast dishes.

They should then write the words to be reviewed against the times, as they find appropriate.

Variation 3

Ask each student to draw a map of their district, and to mark on it one or more of the routes they regularly follow (for example, to work, to school, to a friend's house). On this map they should then place the words to be reviewed.

Comments

Placing words or ideas to be remembered in your house or along your high street is one of the oldest memory techniques known. It was this that was used by Shereshevskii, the prodigious memory man studied in A. R. Luria. *The Mind of a Mnemonist*. Penguin, 1975.

11.5 Leaping words

Level Beginner to advanced

Time 10–15 minutes

Aims To get students to 'draw' words as a simple but creative way of remembering vocabulary visually.

Procedure

1. Ask the students to choose 15 words they find hard to remember from the last few pages of their vocabulary notebooks. They should check them through with a neighbour or you and/or a dictionary.
2. They should now rewrite the words using the shapes and sizes of the letters to bring out the meanings.
3. Ask them to get up and move around the room to show their designs to as many people as possible, explaining why they see particular words thus.

Example In one group *spit* was written

by one student, and *jealousy* as a spiral by another:

Acknowledgements

We first learnt this technique from Michael Legutke, Germany.

11.6 Find the word a picture

Level Beginner to advanced

Time 20–40 minutes

Aims To get students to link words and visual images.

Materials Word cards; a collection of magazine pictures (see Preparation).

Preparation

Select 60 words from the work done during previous classes that need revising. Put each word on a separate card. Select 100 pictures or parts of pictures from magazines. (Rather than select the pictures one by one, it is much more effective, as well as less time-consuming, to keep a box of unsorted pictures (or parts of pictures) cut from magazines etc., and then grab a handful whenever you need them. Try to get your students to add to the box: that way your own tastes will not restrict the variety.)

Procedure

1 Give out the word cards to the students: if you have twenty students, each will get three cards; if thirty, each will get two.

2 Spread the magazine pictures on flat surfaces round the room. Ask the students to get up and circulate. Their task is to find a picture that somehow matches each of their words. It is up to them to decide how. Tell them that the picture doesn't have to illustrate the word *directly*, but may symbolize it, or be suggested by it through association with context or setting. You should be available to help students who don't remember their words.

3 Ask the students to explain to each other how they have matched their words and pictures. Each should talk to at least five other people.

Examples Here are some examples of links students found between words and pictures and the explanations they gave:

Words	Pictures	Explanations
rage	a policeman violently carrying off a small child	'It makes me angry.'
a well	a man drowning under a bridge	
hostility	people in a poor quarter jeering at an armed policeman	
forger	plush, shiny cushions on a settee	'Because the leather looks false.'
guilt	a girl running across a street	'Because she feels guilt.'
sprocket	mother holding two young children	'They look as close as a sprocket is to a wheel.'

11.7 Rhyming review

Level Elementary to advanced

Time 20–30 minutes

Aims To provide a simple auditory review of vocabulary, which also focuses on pronunciation and spelling.

Materials Word cards (see Preparation).

Preparation

Choose 10–15 words and put each on a separate card.

Procedure

1 Each student is given a word card and asked to think of a word that rhymes with it. Suppose the word on the card is *mess*. Student A might choose *guess*. A then says: 'The word on my card rhymes with *guess*.'

2 The other students in the group then have to discover what the word on A's card is. They do this by asking questions, rather than simply shouting out the words they think of, for example,

B: *Is it something a girl wears?*
A: *No, it isn't dress.*
C: *Is it something people who live in cities feel a lot?*
A: *No, not stress.*
D: *Is it what a priest does?*
A: *No, not bless.*

3 Repeat steps 1 and 2 as often as you wish, giving a new card to a different student each time.

Acknowledgements

The idea for this activity came from Hurwitz and Goddard. *Games to Improve Your Child's English.* Kaye and Ward, 1972.

11.8 Draw the word

Level Beginner to advanced

Time 5 minutes in the first class, 15–20 minutes in the second.

Aims To get students to visualize words as a means of remembering them.

Preparation

Choose the words you want the students to review. There is no reason why these should only be ones that can be easily drawn.

Procedure

Lesson 1

Put the words on the board, then tell the students to draw a picture for each word as homework.

Lesson 2

Ask the students to work in pairs, simultaneously, showing their drawings to each other and explaining why they feel the drawings fit the words.

Example

interregnum	One king dead on the ground and another alive, about to be crowned.
replacement	One person handing a bag to another.
to receive	A bricklayer receiving a brick from a helper.
to reach	A person trying to get something from the top of a high cupboard.
emphasize	A teacher at a blackboard underlining two words.
desire	A cyclist gazing at a van. (The student explained that this was the cyclist's desire for the van.)
exclusive	A house surrounded by high walls and locked gates.
skill	A potter making a vase on a wheel.
observation	A fire-watching tower in a forest.
to develop	A child at various stages of growth from infancy.

Variation

1. Write the words on the blackboard in arbitrary pairs.
2. Ask the students, working individually, to draw pictures linking the words in each pair.
3. *Either* ask the students to show their pictures to one or two neighbours and explain the links shown; *or* form groups of four to five students. In each group, all the pictures should be pooled, and one by one individuals should take a picture from the pool and try to guess the words represented and the links between them.

Comments

Students who 'cannot draw' may benefit more than those who can, as they will need to find words to explain their drawings.

11.9 Matching words

Level **Elementary to advanced**

Time **15–30 minutes**

Aims **To review words, focusing on meaning and context.**

Materials **30 word cards and 30 definitions cards (see Preparation).**

Preparation

Select not more than thirty words that need reviewing. Put each one on a separate card. For each word find a synonym, opposite, dictionary definition, or 'groping definition' (see *honesty* below) and put one of these on a card, so that you end up with thirty cards that match the thirty word cards.

Here are examples for four words:

word cards	matching cards	
tact	diplomacy	(synonym)
bravery	cowardice	(opposite)
elegance	the quality of being refined or graceful	(dictionary definition)
honesty	it begins with 'h'— but the 'h' isn't sounded— you can trust someone who has it—they won't lie to you	(groping definition)

Procedure

1 Give each student one or two of the word cards and one or two of the matching cards (depending on class size) and ask them to get up and mill around the room trying to find cards to match their own. Ask them to note down who has the cards corresponding to theirs, and what is on them (this reduces chaos).

2 Ask a student to call out one of their words: the person with the matching card then calls out the matching word or definition. This goes on until all the cards have been matched.

Variation

The preparation outlined above takes quite a bit of time. Why do it yourself? Simply choose the words you want revised (or ask the students to choose) and ask a more advanced group to provide the synonyms, opposites and definitions to put on card. They will be delighted to know their work is being put to a directly practical use.

Acknowledgements

Mike Lavery gave us the outline of this exercise. The idea of using 'groping definitions' has been used in M. Berer and M. Rinvolucri. *Mazes*. Heinemann, 1981.

11.10 Gift words

Level Beginner to advanced

Time 20 minutes

Aims To review vocabulary and at the same time to establish or improve rapport within a group.

Procedure

1 Ask the students to pick out 20 words they feel need reviewing from recent work and to check they know what they mean.

2 Tell them to put the words each on a slip of paper, and to write on each slip the name of a person in the group for whom the word would be an appropriate gift.

3 Everyone now gets up and mills around giving the words away. If the receiver of a word does not understand it, the giver should explain the meaning, and the reason for the gift.

Variation

Half the class sit with their word slips spread out in front of them. The other half move round taking the words they feel they would like and explaining why.

Acknowledgements

This exercise is a transposition of an activity used in therapy and proposed by Ted Saretsky in *Active Techniques and Group Psychotherapy*. Jason Aronson, 1977.

11.11 Forced choice

Level Elementary to advanced

Time 15–25 minutes

Aims To generate conversation by a fast and energetic review of words.

Preparation

Choose half a dozen pairs of words from a vocabulary area to be revised, so that there is an opposition within each pair. If, for example, you want students to review 'water words', you might choose these pairs:

spring – well
estuary – waterfall
drowning – floating
starfish – whale
lake – river
sprinkler – goggles

Procedure

1 Get all the students standing in the middle of the room. Tell them you are going to offer them a choice: they are going to have to choose which thing they think they are most like. If you are working with *water* you might say:

People who think they are like a spring must go to that end of the room—people who think they are like a well must go to the other end of the room.

Oblige any fence-sitters to choose one end of the room.

2 Now ask the people to talk to their neighbours in pairs and explain why they chose as they did. Insist that they work in pairs, not clusters of three or more. Set a time-limit of no more than one minute for each exchange.

3 Ask students from one end of the room to go over and talk to the people who made the opposite choice.

4 Repeat Steps 1, 2, and 3 with a new pair of words.

Acknowledgements

We learnt this technique from S.B. Simon, Howe and Kirschenbaum. *Values Clarification.* Hart Co. 1979.

11.12 Question and answer

Level Elementary to advanced

Time 15–25 minutes

Aims To practise the vocabulary under review interactively and in new contexts.

Materials One word card for each student (see Preparation).

Preparation

Select 30–40 words that need reviewing. Prepare cards with ten words on each. Every student will need to be given one ten-word card.

Procedure

1 Pair the students. Give each person a card and ensure that partners have different cards.

2 Student A must not show their card to student B. Student A looks at the first word on the card and asks B a question aimed at getting B to say the word. If A's question does not elicit from B the word on A's card, A fires more questions until B says the word. This is how it can go:

The first word on A's card is *invasion*.

A: *What did the Americans do to Vietnam?*
B: *Bombed it?*
A: *Yes ... and what have the Israelis often done to Lebanon?*
B: *Attacked it?*
A: *What do you say when one country moves an army into another?*
B: *It invades it.*
A: *What's the noun for that?*
B: *'Invasion'.*

3 B does the same to A. They alternate until all the words on both cards have been dealt with.

Acknowledgements

We found this technique in Byrne and Rixon (Eds.). *Communication Games.* ELT Guide 1, Second edition. NFER Publishing Co. 1982.

11.13 Words to story

Level Elementary to advanced
Time 20–30 minutes
Aims To use oral storytelling to review words.

Preparation

Choose 30–40 words that need revising.

Procedure

1 Put up the words on the board or overhead projector. Ask the students to check any words they don't remember the meaning of.

2 Ask individual students to pick six or seven words from those on the board.

3 Each student then makes up a story (mentally, not on paper) suggested by the words they have chosen.

4 The students pair off and tell each other their stories, then explain how they chose those particular words.

11.14 Word rush

Level Beginner to intermediate
Time 10 minutes
Aims To review words in an energetic, non-wordy way.
Materials Word cards (see Preparation).

Preparation

Put 20 words to be reviewed each on a separate card.

Procedure

1 Divide the class into two teams, A and B. Have the two teams assemble at one end of the classroom. Go to the other end yourself.

2 Call out a member of each team and show them one word.

3 Each team member rushes back to their team and *draws* or *mimes* the word. They must not write, speak, or whisper! The first team that recognizes the word from the drawing and shouts it out correctly gets a point.

Acknowledgements

The activity comes from Viola Spolin's goldmine of drama ideas, *Improvisation for the Theatre*. Pitman, 1963.

11.15 Comparing random words

Level Elementary to advanced

Time 5 minutes in the first lesson; 15 minutes in the second lesson.

Aims To provide a somewhat surreal way of reviewing 'hard-to-remember' words.

Procedure

Lesson 1

For homework, ask the students to go back over the last five units of the coursebook, and each pick out ten words they find it hard to remember the meaning of. They should put each of these words on a separate slip of paper and bring the slips to their next class.

Lesson 2

1 Check that the students do know the meanings of the words they have put on their slips of paper. Spread all the slips face down over the teacher's desk.

2 Take two slips at random and make a comparative sentence about them and put it up on the board. If the two words are *beyond* and *camel*, you might write:
The camel feels further away than beyond.
or
The camel is more real than beyond.

3 Ask the students, one at a time, to come to the front, pick two words, make a comparative sentence about them and put the sentence up on the board.

4 Stop when the board is full.

Comments

If students cannot remember a word, then the chances are that either the word or the context(s) in which it has been met failed to engage their attention.

Acknowledgements

We learnt this activity from a Chandler and Stone article we found on the Web at http://www.etprofessional.com/

11.16 Multi-sensory revision

Level Elementary to advanced

Time 30–40 minutes

Aims To get students to choose whether to revise linguistically, kinaesthetically, auditorily or visually.

Procedure

1 Ask the students to go back over the past three units in the coursebook and each pull out ten words they find hard to remember or have already forgotten the meaning of.

2 Have a secretary come to the board: the students dictate their words to the secretary, who writes them here and there over the board.

3 Propose these four ways the students can revise the words:

a Write the words out in a sequence so that the last letter of word 1 is the same as the first letter of word 2, for example: *egg... go... otter...* etc. Add extra words if really necessary.

b Think about each word and imagine it through your body, for example:

rain: you feel the wet on your skin
betrayal: you get the feeling of emptiness turning to anger.

Write down the word and the association.

c Associate the word to be remembered with a word of similar sound, so if the phrase to remember is *football pitch*, you might come up with *foolish witch*. Do this for all the words. Jot down the sound-associated words.

d Get a picture in your mind of the idea behind each word to be remembered. Write down one word to remind you of each picture.

4 Allow the students 10–15 minutes to work their way through the words, whichever way they wish.

5 Ask the students which way they chose to work on the word (a, b, c, or d). Group all the a's, all the b's, all the c's, and all the d's, and within these groupings have the students work in threes or fours to describe what they did with the words.

6 The first time you use this exercise, allow time for plenary feedback.

Comments

This activity allows the student to choose whether to revise linguistically, kinaesthetically, auditorily, or visually. (See the introduction to Chapter 6.) If you use the exercise more than once, encourage students to try more than one way.

Acknowledgements

We came across the above four ways of revising words in William Holden's article 'Learning to Learn', in *Modern English Teacher* 8/2, 1999.

11.17 Writing to rule

Level Elementary to advanced

Time 30–40 minutes

Aims To encourage students to extract as much meaning as they can from words by limiting the number they are allowed to use.

Procedure

1 Tell the students they are going to be writing a 50-word story. Ask them to decide whether they prefer to work alone or in pairs, and to sit accordingly.

2 Now tell them that they are to write *exactly* 50 words and that no word may be repeated, not even the articles, helping verbs, etc.

3 As they write, help, when requested, with the language problems the 'no repetition' rule imposes.

4 Group the students in sixes to enjoy listening to each other's stories. Tell them to listen critically just in case there has been an unwitting repetition.

Variations

1 Experiment with different word counts: is 30 words too short, or 100 words too long?

2 Relax the restriction on articles, common verbs, etc. Does this make the activity more or less creative?

3 Invent, or get the students to invent, other restrictions, such as limiting the number of times specific words, sounds, or letters may be used, or banning (or insisting on) specific words (*and, I, not, …*).

Comments

Rules, even, or perhaps especially, arbitrary ones, can stimulate and encourage as well as restrict a writer. If, for example, your students block when you ask them 'Write three sentences using these words', tell them to make the sentences exactly eleven words long.

Acknowledgements

We found this activity in Michael Lewis (1993). The parlour and radio game *Just a Minute* asks players to speak on a theme for exactly one minute 'without hesitation, repetition, or deviation'. The 'mini-sagas' popularized in Britain by the *Daily Telegraph* are stories of exactly 50 words, but may include repetition.

Annotated bibliography

Aitchison, Jean. 1994. *Words in the Mind: An Introduction to the Mental Lexicon* Second edition. Oxford: Blackwell.

Words and how we learn, remember, understand, and find the ones we want. The author discusses the structure and content of the human word-store or 'mental lexicon'.

Ashton-Warner, Sylvia. 1963. *Teacher*. London: Secker and Warburg.

Experiences of a teacher in New Zealand, with remarkable insight into children's motivations to learn.

Augarde, Tony. 2003. *Oxford Guide to Word Games*. Second edition. Oxford: Oxford University Press.

Examines twenty-six forms of word game including Scrabble and Spoonerisms, crosswords and chronograms, riddles and puns, describing their history and social context.

Ayto, John. 1999. *Twentieth-Century Words*. Oxford: Oxford University Press.

A unique retrospective of the twentieth century providing insight into the development of the English language decade by decade, with around 5000 new words and usages.

Baker, Mona. 1992. *In Other Words: a Coursebook on Translation.* London: Routledge.

Addresses the need for a systematic approach to training in translation studies by exploring various areas of language and relating the theoretical findings to the actual practice of translation.

Bandler, Richard and **John Grinder.** 1975. *The Structure of Magic*. Palo Alto: Science and Behavior Books.

Subtitled 'Language and therapy', it defines those predictable elements that make change happen in language-based transactions.

Bateson, Gregory. 1973. *Steps to an Ecology of Mind*. Boulder, Co.: Paladin Books.

Collected essays in anthropology, psychiatry, evolution and much else that goes to make up Bateson's view of the mind as a network of interactions relating the individual with his society.

Bateson, Gregory. 1991. *A Sacred Unity: Further Steps to an Ecology of Mind.* London: HarperCollins.

A second volume of collected essays.

Burbidge, Nicky, Peta Gray, Sheila Levy, and **Mario Rinvolucri.** 1996. *Letters*. Oxford: Oxford University Press. (in this series)

Campbell, Linda, Bruce Campbell, and **Dee Dickinson.** 1998.*Teaching and Learning Through Multiple Intelligences*. Second edition. New York: Pearson. Allyn and Bacon.

Practical, workable ideas based on Gardner's theories. The second edition contains materials based on the 'latest intelligences'.

Collins Cobuild. 1998. *Grammar Patterns 1: Verbs*. London: HarperCollins.

Based on the the Cobuild corpus.

Deller, Sheelagh and **Mario Rinvolucri.** 2002. *Using the Mother Tongue*. ETp-Delta.

Provides ideas and guidelines on when and how to use the mother tongue not just for convenience but as a real, living, and vital resource.

Freire, Paulo. 1972. *Cultural Action for Freedom.* Harmondsworth: Penguin Books.

The cultural and political power of words, in the context of adult literacy programmes.

Gairns, Ruth and **Stuart Redman.** 1986. *Working with Words*. Cambridge: Cambridge University Press.

The first systematic theoretical treatment of vocabulary acquisition.

Gardner, Howard. 1999a. *Intelligence Reframed: Multiple Intelligences for the 21st Century.* New York: Basic Books.
A progress report on how the theory of multiple intelligences has evolved since it was first set forth in Howard Gardner's 1983 book *Frames of Mind*.

Gardner, Howard. 1999b. *The Disciplined Mind: What All Students Should Understand.* New York: Simon and Schuster.
A synthesis of Gardner's ideas aimed at parents, educators, and the general public alike. The book explores the larger questions of what an educated person should be and how such an education can be achieved.

Haley, Jay. (ed.). 1985. *Conversations with Milton H. Erickson* Volumes 1–3. New York: Triangle Press.
Volume 1 *Changing Individuals*, Volume 2 *Changing Couples*, and Volume 3 *Changing Children and Families* all explore Erickson's contribution to therapy as various kinds of linguistic intervention to bring about change.

Knowles, Elizabeth (ed.). 1997. *The Oxford Dictionary of New Words*. Second edition. Oxford: Oxford University Press.
The story of around 2000 words and phrases prominent in the media or the public eye in the 1980s and 1990s.

Lewis, Michael. 1993. *The Lexical Approach*. Hove: Language Teaching Publications.
The book's main principles are that language consists of grammaticalized lexis not lexicalized grammar. Methods, materials and teacher training are discussed.

Meara, Paul. 1997. 'Towards a new approach to modelling vocabulary acquisition' in Schmitt, N. and M.J. McCarthy (eds.). *Vocabulary: Description, Acquisition and Pedagogy*. Cambridge: Cambridge University Press.
Discusses the Key Word approach.

McCarthy, Michael. 1998. *Spoken Language and Applied Linguistics.* Cambridge: Cambridge University Press.
Gives a central role to the spoken language in the syllabus. It brings together a number of separate studies by the author, based on the CANCODE spoken corpus.

O'Connor, Joseph and **John Seymour.** 1990. *Introducing NLP*. London: HarperCollins.
Describes what good communicators do differently, and enables the reader to learn these patterns of excellence.

Orage, A. R. 1998. *On Love and Psychological Exercises*. York Beach, Maine: Samuel Weiser.
A collection of essays from the long-time editor of the magazine *New Age*. First published in London, 1930.

Raudsepp, Eugene. 1977. *Creative Growth Games*. New York: Perigee Books/Putnam.
A collection of 75 games to expand creativity and make you think.

Silver, Harvey F., Richard W. Strong, and **Matthew J. Perini**. 2000. *So Each May Learn: Integrating Learning Styles and Multiple Intelligences*. Alexandria, Va.: Association for Supervision and Curriculum Development.
Rationales and research-based principles of learning that support integrated learning to help educators process ideas and analyse their current practices; includes instruments for identifying style and intelligence profiles.

Spolin, Viola. 1963. *Improvisation for the Theatre*. London: Pitman.
Spolin worked with students and professionals in the theatre, but extended this to elementary and secondary education—from gifted students to children with severe learning disabilities.

Stevick, Earl. 1996. *Memory, Meaning and Method.* Rowley, Mass.: Newbury House.
Particularly good as a survey of views on memory and vocabulary retention.

Stevick, Earl. 1980. *A Way and Ways*. Rowley, Mass.: Newbury House.
An excellent survey of 'new' methods in language teaching.

Wahl, Mark. 1999. *Math for Humans: Teaching Math Through 8 Intelligences*. Langley, Wash.: LivnLern Press.
An introduction to and many practical examples of using a broad, multiple intelligences approach to the teaching of mathematics.

Wright, Jon. 1998. *Dictionaries*. Oxford: Oxford University Press. (in this series)
Makes learners aware of the wealth of information in most ELT dictionaries. Practises reading skills, memory training, and encourages learners to 'have fun with dictionaries'.

Concordance software and online resources

Collins Cobuild
http://titania.cobuild.collins.co.uk
Offers a free trial use of a section of the 'Bank of English' corpus, with concordances limited to 40 hits.

Copernic query engine. http://www.copernic.com
Powerful, generalized search and query software.

Dodd, Tony. *SARA-32.* Search software for the *British National Corpus, World Edition.* Humanities Computing Unit, Oxford University.
http://www.hcu.ox.ac.uk/BNC
Free trial available. Will give you 50 hits from the 100 million-word British National Corpus.

Lee, David. http://devoted.to/corpora
Frequently updated corpus website reporting on new developments in corpora and concordance software.

Scott, Mike. *Wordsmith Tools.*
http://www.oup.co.uk or
http://www.oup.com/elt/global/catalogue/multimedia
Probably the most powerful, versatile and learner-centric corpus tools available.

Watts, R. J. C. *Concordance.*
http://www.rjcw.freeserve.co.uk
Text analysis and concordancing software used in a wide range of subject areas.

Dictionaries and thesauri online and CD-ROMS

Collins bilingual dictionaries (Spanish, German, Italian, French):
http://www.wordreference.com/

Lexical FreeNet Thesaurus: http://www.lexfn.com

Oxford English Dictionary Online.
http://www.oed.com/

Oxford Phrasebuilder Genie. CD-ROM. Oxford University Press.
Collocational dictionary which integrates with your word processor and web browser.

Plumb Design. *Visual Thesaurus.*
http://www.visualthesaurus.com

Roget's Thesaurus.
http://www.bartleby.com/thesauri
http://www.gutenberg.net

Crossword software

Beresford, Ross. *TEA & Sympathy.*
http://bryson.ltd.uk

Casson, Henry. *Crossword Utility.*
http://home.freeuk.net/dharrison/puzzles/utility.htm

Crossword Compiler 6. http://www.crossword-puzzle-maker.com

Crossword Maestro. http://www.genius2000.com

Index

In the general index references are to page numbers; in the Topics and Language indexes references are to activity numbers. Some terms may appear in more than one index.

General index

Topics

Language